GW00385265

JAMES FINTAN LALOR: RADICAL

James F. Lalor

James Fintan Lalor: Radical

By

DAVID N. BUCKLEY

Cork University Press

1990

First published in 1990 by
Cork University Press, University College, Cork
in collaboration with the
Irish Studies Program, Boston College

British Library Cataloguing in Publication Data
Buckley, David
James Fintan Lalor: radical.
1. Ireland. Land tenure. Lalor, James Finton
I. Title
333.323092

ISBN 0-902561-56-1

Typeset and printed in the Republic of Ireland by
Tower Books, 39 Lavitts Quay, Cork

For my father
Michael James Buckley (1911-1987)
and my mother
Ellen Buckley (nee McCarthy) (1916-1980)
who made the miracle of 'free' education
available to me

Contents

Preface

Lalor is a marginal character in the history of nineteenth-century Ireland; yet, paradoxically, he appears at the very centre of all accounts of the age. Because his brief public career spanned the nightmare years from 1847 to 1849 — at the height of the famine, and in the limbo between the collapse of Repeal/Young Ireland and the emergence of a unified Tenant Right movement — general histories of the period have invariably used him as a convenient pedagogical hinge on which to mark the transition from pre-famine to post-famine politics. Thus, his marginal involvement in a variety of movements in the late 1840s, paradoxically, puts him at the center of Irish history!

However, far too great returns are expected from so simple a rhetorical turn. For instance, Lalor's public insistence on the fundamental importance of the land question, both in his letters to *The Nation* and in his attempts to organize the tenants of Tipperary in 1847, is often paraded not only as a welcome antidote to Young Ireland's absurd social romanticism, but also as a long-overdue return to a more realistic, 'grassroots', 'bread-and-butter' politics. This, clearly, overstates the case. Granted, he was a positive influence on the Tenant Right League in the 1850s; yet, in his broader political goals, he had more in common with Young Ireland's ardent nationalism than with the League's narrow, self-serving pragmatism. In addition, though he championed the cause of tenant farmers, this hardly made him a Jeffersonian republican in the midst of Young Ireland's royalists. Finally, whilst it is true that his involvement in the secret societies of '49 justifies our seeing him as a precursor of the Fenians, yet a more tangible influence than this is surely needed if we are seriously to consider them his heirs.

Clearly, too insistent an emphasis on his multifarious political activities subverts any attempt to provide a coherent, unifying interpretation of his brief public career. For, if his links to contemporary movements are to be taken as definitive badges of his political beliefs, how can we avoid having several different Lalors — each at the mercy of his latter-day disciples? Did he not have any convictions of his own, independent of the opinions of his peers and colleagues, and did these not influence his actions? Unfortunately, traditional answers to such questions have depended less on Lalor's ideas than on the ideological convictions of his interpreters. This, inevitably, has spawned even more Lalors — Lalor the Nationalist, and Lalor the Socialist, being foremost among them.

I have tried, in the study that follows, to rescue Lalor from the pitfalls of both of these approaches. By reversing the traditional, textbook emphasis on his activities, (which implies that he acted always under the pressure of events) and focusing instead on his writings, I have attempted to demonstrate the extent to which his politics were informed and illuminated by his ideas. Avoiding the pitfalls of ideological canonization, however, has proved more difficult. Simply to assert that I have not been motivated by any desire to claim him as a precursor for this or that group, is hardly an adequate defence against the possible imputation of special pleading. I have, therefore, taken refuge in a rigorously critical, though I hope not uncharitable, scrutiny of his ideas. The results may not endear him to his disciples, but they do, at least, reassert the historical intimacy of text and context.

It defies explanation that so modest a work can have acquired so many debts. Chief among them are those I owe Professor J.J. Lee, who encouraged me to research and write this topic as a Master's thesis, almost a decade ago, in University College, Cork. Intent as I was (then as now) on researching the *culs-de-sac*, I might never have discovered the main street were it not for his constant, patient advice and criticism. If my perception of that thoroughfare appears at times disjointed, the fault, of course, is my own. Patience and helpful criticism could not induce me to discard my peculiar spectacles.

My thanks are also due to the faculty of both the Department of Modern History and the Department of Irish History at UCC, for the trouble they took to criticise and discuss an earlier version of the thesis, (presented in a Post-Graduate Seminar under the supervision of Dr Mara Kühne O' Leary). I am particularly indebted to Dr Tom Dunne, not only for his contributions on that occasion, but also for his continuing interest in this work. Having first solicited the thesis for possible inclusion in Tower Books' 'New Perspectives' series, so ably anchored by his own work on Tone, he refused to abandon it when the economic squeeze of the '80s forced reconsideration. He continued to investigate the alternatives, provided much-needed moral support, and graced successive revisions with a light editorial touch. Were it not for his persistence and encouragement, this publication would not have been possible.

Grateful thanks are also due to Prof. Kevin O'Neill and Prof. Adele

Dalsimer, who have now put me doubly in their debt. As the able and energetic Co-Directors of the Irish Studies Programme at Boston College, they have not only made it possible for me to undertake Doctoral studies at Boston College, but they have also provided a generous grant in aid of publication of this work. Their kindness will, I hope, be rewarded by even greater collaboration between the two Universities in the future.

I wish also to thank the librarians and staffs of the following institutions, where much of the original research was undertaken: College Library, UCC; Cork City Library; Cork County Library; Trinity College Library; and the National Library of Ireland. In revising the manuscript for publication I have relied on the extensive Irish holdings in the O'Neill Library at Boston College.

Grateful thanks are also due, for their patience and professionalism, to Donal J. Counihan and his staff at Cork University Press; and to Winifred Murphy for the sketch of Lalor on the dust-jacket.

In Ireland, as elsewhere, working-class people seldom make it to University. Those that do acquire special debts not shared by their more fortunate peers. It is with pleasure, therefore, that I acknowledge the encouragement and support I have always received from my brothers and sisters. Were all Irish children truly cherished equally by the State, my siblings might have pursued their own education, instead of supporting mine. I also owe a special word of thanks to my wife Ann, who first convinced me that I should go to College, and whose astute sociological critiques of my methods, motives and findings has enormously improved the worth of the present study.

Finally, in offering this book by way of posthumous repayment of debts, I have no doubt that those friends to whom it is dedicated would have understood my motives, though they might legitimately have expected something more tangible. I can only hope they would have accepted.

David N. Buckley,
Boston College,
June 1989

Introduction

> Mr Lalor's home was crowded with vigorous sons, fit for all the sports and labours of country life. But the eldest was a painful exception: he was deaf, near-sighted, ungainly, and deformed; and his deficiencies cut him off not only from any career needing sympathy and publicity, but even from social intercourse except with his nearest kin.[1]

Gavan Duffy's political history of Young Ireland, written almost forty years after the demise of that movement, is a useful though highly personalised treatment of the period. It is, on that account, as much a source of confusion as of information and warrants the most careful handling. Necessarily subjective in its judgements of events and personalities it tends, at the expense of others, to reflect most credit on those whom Duffy most avidly supported. Thus, for example, O'Connell's career becomes a foil for a fuller treatment of Davis's intellectual integrity and political vision; Lalor is used as a weapon whereby Mitchel, Doheny, and Reilly ('a vigorous and gifted *boy*, who had not reached the years of discretion')[2] can be cut down to size; and the numerous Confederation debates and divisions on matters of principle, expediency and policy are dutifully (if humbly) paraded as evidence of Duffy's unenviable role as peace-keeper-in-chief, of his hapless position as the sole champion of sound common sense and the best interests of 'the people'.

In particular, his usefulness as a source for Fintan Lalor's background and career are suspect; not least because both men met each other for the first time in Newgate Prison, almost two years after their first exchange of letters in January 1847. Though he later confessed himself amazed by the 'freshness and force'[3] of Lalor's first epistle, he was ill-placed to serve as a reliable witness to the character or integrity of a man whose theories he profoundly distrusted, and on whose background he possessed only a tissue of factual information. Both of these failings he flimsily camouflaged by a fanciful account of Lalor's erstwhile anonymity:

> he was trained by *solitary meditation*, to a concentration and savage earnestness which often distinguish men to whom the ordinary channels of communication are closed; and he was endowed with a will and a persuasiveness of prodigious force. Of all the men who have preached revolutionary politics in Ireland, *this isolated*

thinker, who had hitherto had no experience either as a writer or as an actor in public affairs, was the most original and intense. His imagination was so vivid that his desires framed themselves like palpable images in his mind, and *he lived in a world of dreams* far more real to him than the world that lay about him on an Irish farm. *He projected, as solitary thinkers are apt to do, in the unfenced field of fancy,* and his schemes seemed so logically exact and demonstrable that he could discern no difficulties which forbade their immediate execution.[4]

The obvious shortcomings of Duffy's account are, almost inevitably, reflected in later treatments of Lalor's life. Lack of biographical data, sometimes compounded by factual inaccuracies (as, for example, Standish O'Grady's reference to those theories which 'full-formed, clear, mature, clad as if in shining armour, and equipped for war', sprang from 'the brooding brain of the *Tipperary* recluse'[5]; or John Mitchel's treatment of 'James Fintan Lalor, of *Kildare* county'[6]), was but one aspect of the confusion surrounding Lalor's life and career. A second, and in many respects more serious source of error was the wrangle concerning Lalor's ideological credentials. The careers of Davitt, Pearse, and Connolly, and their individual treatments of Lalor's ideas, gave rise to a debate — replete with rather more heat than light — on the respective vices, virtues, and pedigrees of Socialism and Nationalism in Ireland. Partisans of party purity on both sides laid claim to Lalor's ideas, and ransacked his writings for quotations to prove his pedigree. Unfortunately the individuals involved in the debate were less interested in the integrity of the prophet they were attempting to press-gang into service and subservience, than in the necessity of having him toe the 'party' line. As a result, though the debate tells us a great deal about the political temper of the time, it tells us little or nothing of importance about Lalor, whose career and ideas — now hopelessly dismembered by rival factions — recede even further from our view.

Both aspects of this confusion — the lack of reliable biographical data, and the inability to determine Lalor's importance due to wrangles over his alleged ideological leanings — were created and fostered mainly, if not exclusively, by Duffy. In dealing with Lalor's use of class terminology, for instance, he wrote: 'to propose the scientific organisation of the whole nation by classes to a country in the condition of Ireland at the time [1840s], was like advising protoplasm to get itself a spine and muscles.'[7] Obviously this critique was less a realistic assessment of Lalor's political and social theories of the 1840s, than a reflection of Duffy's reaction to the politics of the '70s and '80s. In fact, as we shall see, Duffy too had availed of class, and other conflict theories, when dealing with the crisis of famine.

With one eye on the politics of the 1890s, John O'Leary — though he provides additional information on Lalor's career — similarly embroils himself in a discussion of 'the relative merits of our Irish classes and our Irish masses'. In fact, whilst he excuses himself 'from saying all, or nearly all, that I could about [Lalor]', on the grounds that his book is about fenians and fenianism, he seizes every available opportunity to address himself to questions which are more relevant to his prospective audience than to an understanding of 'this very remarkable, but now little-known man'. In giving his account of the events of the late 1840s, O'Leary admits the possibility that he personally 'had taken some tinge of agrarianism in '48, no doubt from the writings of Mitchel, and still more of Lalor himself'. Nevertheless, at the time of writing (1895) he is anxious to put as much distance as possible between himself and 'Lalor's peculiar theories on the land question'.[8]

Even John Savage, who knew Lalor for a time in 1849, does not rise above the temptation to categorise him ideologically: 'he was ever a revolutionist', he declared. 'A true patriot, a passionate hater of tyranny under any form of sky, he died a relentless *Republican*.'[9] Where the expert witnesses are slow to provide biographical detail, and all too swift in providing ideological tags and justifications, it is perhaps inevitable that the secondary sources should share the same failings. Thus, T.J. O'Donohue in his introduction to one of the earliest editions (1895) of Lalor's writings, acknowledged the fact that 'Of [Lalor's] life very little is known'; yet, despite the paucity of reliable information, he confidently declared Fintan 'an ardent Republican' and 'an uncompromising Nationalist'.[10] Two decades later, in an additional collection of Lalor's writings, Nathaniel Marlowe coupled his misinformed claim that Fintan 'was married and left a son, who was afterwards a member of Parliament' with the dogmatic assertion that: 'He certainly did not write at that time as an advocate of Socialism, or of any proposal for the nationalization of land; he wrote as a Nationalist.'[11] In the same year (1918), Arthur Griffith was proclaiming in a rival edition of Lalor's collected writings: 'Essentially Lalor was a Land Reformer rather than a Nationalist.'[12] By then, however, any hope of rescuing Lalor from his admirers was virtually impossible as Pearse and Connolly, the two leading ideologues of Nationalism and Socialism respectively — and both of whom had appropriated Lalor in one guise or another, as a forebear — had been executed for their part in the rebellion of 1916.

Connolly's Socialist Party of Ireland, in fact, had earlier published a pamphlet of Lalor's writings prefaced by the following remarks:

> The Socialist Party of Ireland stands today in much the same position as Fintan Lalor occupied in '48. Indeed a most striking parallel exists between his time and our own. In '48 there stood on the one side the landlords backed up by the government in demanding their rents, while the people were left to starve in the midst of plenty. On the other side, there stood, nominally in opposition to the government, the two sections of the Repeal Party. Of these two sections, one, the Repeal Association, was tame, constitutional, and time-serving, its only hope being to secure the good offices of middle-class English politicians, repealers and repealers only. The other section, the Confederation, intelligent, honest and sincere, according to their lights, but (with a few exceptions, such as John Mitchel) like the first, thoroughly conservative on the really fundamental question of property, firm believers in rent, interest and profit, outvying even the government in their insistence on the landlord's right to his rent, also repealers only, but, under a multitude of grandiloquent phrases hiding even from themselves the utter paltriness of our ideal. Today we have in our midst the same story repeated. In the Home Rule camp again exist two opposing sections, the most advanced of whom are as hopelessly conservative as ever in their opposition to the claim of the labourer to the full produce of his toil. Under these circumstances, The Socialist Party of Ireland [is] the only political party in Ireland which fully accepts Fintan Lalor's teaching, from his declaration of principles to his system of insurrection.[13]

Connolly does not attempt to explain, what is patently implied: that 'Lalor's teaching' differed in important respects 'on the really fundamental question of property' from that (or those?) of his fellow Confederationists. Despite the contention that Lalor 'died as he had lived, a revolutionist and a rebel against all forms of political and social injustice', Connolly's introductory remarks are less an evaluation or explication of the man or his principles, than a consideration of the historical role of the Socialist Party of Ireland.[14] Though this imbalance was later corrected to some extent in *Labour in Irish history* by a closer treatment of Lalor's tenets,[15] nevertheless the central imbalance remained substantially intact. Connolly's ideological view of the past loomed larger than, and hence tended to swamp, his evaluation of individual actors. In the historical struggle between a primitive, native 'communism' and an imported, or invading, capitalism Lalor was inevitably seen as an ideological pawn.

Pearse, no less than Connolly, had a broad view of the sweep of history — though he saw it as an eschatological rather than an emancipatory process. Perhaps as a result, he portrayed Lalor as a martyred fore-runner, an Evangelist on horseback who had come down trailing clouds of glory and inspiration from God. His 'new gospel', which Pearse considered 'self-luminous', was delivered in 'the ringing voice of an angel'. For Lalor, he declared, was a fiery spirit, as of some angelic missionary, imprisoned for a few years in a very frail tenement, drawing his earthly breath in pain; but strong with a great spiritual strength and gifted with a mind which had the trenchant beauty of steel . . . Commonly, it is by reading and writing that a man learns to write greatly. Lalor, who had read little and written nothing, wrote greatly from the moment he began to write. The Lord God must have inspired the poor crippled recluse, for no mortal man could of himself have uttered the things he uttered.[16]

Obviously, such a view has less to do with the reality of Lalor's situation than with Pearse's peculiar brand of sacred politics and secular religion.

Even Arthur Griffith, who had come extremely close to a full understanding of Lalor's theories, failed to forego the urge to castigate him on the irrelevant grounds that 'he failed to apprehend, as List did, that nationality was the highest value in economics'.[17] The edition for which Griffith wrote these words in 1918 was later to become the standard popular collection of Lalor's writings. The editor, Miss Fogarty, attempted a more complete biographical note than those provided by Gavan Duffy, O'Leary or Savage. However, she too was inclined, in the face of a chilling paucity of reliable data, to repeat Duffy's mistake and invent a persona for Lalor: 'even in boyhood [she wrote], Fintan Lalor was marked apart as one of the solitary ones of earth — his thoughts exploring universes, his footsteps pacing the highways and byways of life, companionless'.[18] By the time a second edition of her collection appeared in 1947, Miss Fogarty had had access to Lalor's private papers (now in the National Library).[19] As a result, she provided a much fuller factual account of Lalor's career and could drop the mask of romantic despair with which she had gratuitously cloaked him some thirty years previously. Though she was at times remiss in acknowledging her sources of information, she had managed to lay — almost a century after Lalor's death — the firm foundations for a complete biographical study. However it was not until 1962 that Tomás Ó Néill's book, *Fiontán Ó Leathlobhair*, reached the public.[20]

Unfortunately, despite the fact that there are still some considerable gaps to be filled in Lalor's career, the advances made in the study of biographical minutiae — pioneered almost exclusively by Miss Fogarty and, later by T.P. Ó Néill — have not in fact succeeded in 'rescuing Lalor from his disciples'.[21] In particular, though Ó Néill's work marked an inestimable advance over everything that had preceded it, it nonetheless compounded rather than resolved the central dilemma of Lalor's career: viz, whether he was a Nationalist or a Socialist. In addition, though Ó Néill's research brought to light a new and important letter which Lalor had written to Peel in 1843 and in which he claimed to be a conservative, Ó Néill's only comment was:

> is beag duine a léann an litir sin den chéad uair ná go mbaineann sí stad as. San am gcéanna ní feidir le héinne a rá nach o chroi mhacánta a scríobhadh í. Ní ag lorg bréibe bhí sé . . .[22]

That Ó Néill should feel compelled to immediately defend Lalor against the possible imputation of being 'on the make' is instructive insofar as it reveals the author's underlying 'philosophy' of history. In addition, by declaring that '*Le linn dó an litir sin a scríobh bhí sé ina Choimeadach sealbhaithe ina chroi istig*',[23] Ó Néill is focusing all-too-readily on the surface politics of the situation. Inevitably, in the final analysis, Lalor is interpreted, despite his earlier political colours, as a Nationalist. This however, is not the only, nor is it (in the eyes of the present writer at least) the best possible interpretation of Lalor's life and career.

1

Lalor's Life: an Interpretation

(i) BACKGROUND AND EARLY LIFE

Lalor's father, Patrick, may have been little more than 'a prosperous tenant farmer'[1] in Queen's County (Laois) when, in 1806, he married Anne Dillon from neighbouring King's County (Offaly). However, within ten years he had firmly established himself as 'a gentleman farmer'[2] with an income of £438-15s-5d from the rent of five houses in Mountrath and of two of his three farms.[3] He ran one of the farms himself and, though an 'improver', was also 'one of the brood of middlemen' — a much criticised breed in this period — 'who lived between the landlords and the *working* tenants'.[4] By 1832, with a family of twelve in his care,[5] he had accumulated 'between six hundred and seven hundred Irish acres' (between 972 and 1,134 statute acres) of which he re-let 'about 100 acres'.[6] Despite the 'very variable quality of land' in the area, Lalor estimated average rents at 'about 25s' per acre, whilst admitting that his own rent 'averages about 30s'.[7] It is not unreasonable to suppose that the £150 which accrued from sub-letting this 100 acres at above average rents was substantially augmented by the returns on the remaining five or six hundred Irish acres, despite his contention that 'in Ireland land is a commodity that is taken as a matter of necessity, not as a speculation for making money'.[8]

In matters political he was a staunch O'Connellite, having taken part in the drive for Catholic Emancipation in the 1820s[9] before his rise to political prominence during the Tithe War. Some fifty years later his son William recalled the meeting in Maryborough (Portlaois) which led to his father's involvement in that agitation:

In speaking to a resolution my father, Patrick (or as he was more generally called, Patt) Lalor, of Tinakill, took occasion to refer to the tithe system; and, in so doing, made the astounding declaration that he would never again pay tithes; that he would violate no law; that the tithe men might take his property, and offer it for sale; but his countrymen, he was proud to say, respected him, and he thought that none of them would buy or bid for it if exposed for sale. The declaration was received by the meeting in various ways: by many with surprise and astonishment; by others with consternation and dismay, but by a vast majority with tremendous cheering. After passing resolutions to get up a petition for reform the meeting dissolved.[10]

In the ensuing struggle, Lalor had twenty-five of his sheep distrained as payment of tithes, but he ensured that they would not be sold at any market in either Ireland or England, by branding their flanks with the word TITHE in large capitals.[11] 'I considered it a debt not morally binding', he explained to the Lords Committee on Tithes in February 1832; for 'if the law allowed the nonpayment of it, I conceive(d) there was no moral obligation to enforce it'.[12] He added that he felt

there was every facility to avoid the payment of tithes, if the people were only unanimous, and acted peaceably, as the society called Quakers did; and it struck me that that time was peculiarly favourable to advance that opinion, and in consequence I made use of the speech, which has been referred to, at Maryborough.[13]

The object and outcome of this Quaker-inspired policy of passive resistance was Boycott or, as Lalor termed it, 'the non-dealing system'.[14] Handbills were posted up in the vicinity quoting his speech, and recommending that 'not the slightest intercourse' be held with anyone who bought distrained goods; nor should anyone 'have anything whatever to do with [such a person], nor . . . give him one hour's labour for love nor money'.

Do you not believe [he was asked by the Lords Committee] that if that recommendation had been attended to any person so treated must have been entirely ruined? — I am sure he would.
Do you not call that a threat? — I would not call it a threat, because I conceive that a threat means personal injury . . .
Do not landlords sometimes threaten tenants with ejectments in the country? — Yes, they do; but, using the word in common parlance, when we speak of threats we mean threats of bodily injury.
In fact you were anxious that the resistance should be made without violent collision, in the way the Quakers have done it? — Yes.[15]

Lalor's activity in mobilising community opprobrium as a political force within the law contained, as Professor MacDonagh says, 'the embryo of civil disobedience which was to be fully grown in the Land League's "No Rent Manifesto" and the Plan of Campaign in the 1880s'.[16] His moral politics, as befits a follower of O'Connell, are carefully tailored to remain within the law. He stresses that 'the best legal advice I could get was, that I could not, under the Tithe-Composition Act, be compelled to pay tithes'.[17] More revealing on this point is the evidence he gave to the House of Commons Committee on Tithes.[18]

Do not you know that the law directs you to pay tithe? — Yes, I do; as all penal laws do; but I conceive that penal laws carry no moral obligation with them . . .
Then your notion is, that it is for each individual person, and not the Legislature, to consider whether the law is binding or not? — So far as his own opinion is concerned, I think so; I think every law is open to be canvassed by the individuals affected by it . . .
When the law says positively, in emphatic terms, you shall pay your tithe to the tithe-owner, does not the person who refuses to pay tithe refuse to obey the plain injunction of the law? — No; because I conceive the law goes further, and says, in case you should refuse or neglect to pay tithes, such and such proceedings shall be had against your person or property; then it gives him the option of either paying the money or allowing the law to take its course.
Do you conceive that you are not breaking the law when you evade the payment, although you do not resist the payment? — I do not think I am.
The law says you shall pay the tithe; then when the demand is made upon you, you refuse to pay; do you then obey the law, or disobey the law? — I think I obey the law in giving no resistance to the law to take its course, which says, that in case you shall refuse or decline to pay this money, so and so shall be the consequences; I think I have the option to take whichever portion of that law I please.[19]

Lalor's arguments exasperated both committees because they regarded the law as absolute and immutable. However, he did not emerge totally unscathed. Both Revd Thomas Stuart Townshend, who held a church preferment in Timogue, and Revd T. Harper, sequestrator of Mountrath, accused him of vested interest of a parochial political nature. Townshend claimed 'that a good deal of the opposition [in Mountrath] arose in consequence of Mr Lalor not having been appointed one of the tithe commissioners; and it was stated that Mr Latouche had promised that he should be so'.[20] In view of the fact that he lumped all 'Roman Catholic farmers' together under the title 'peasant', and held the traditional conspiracy view of all attacks on the besieged privileged classes — 'I am convinced it required a complete system of terror to induce a great portion of the respectable Roman-catholic farmers to fall in with the present system of opposition'[21] — Townshend's evidence may seem, at least, suspect. Harper's accusation that 'Lalor's animosity against the tithe system would have been at least greatly mitigated in the event of his having been appointed a commissioner, which situation I have always understood he anxiously sought after'[22] is certainly not implausible. However, we need not depend on either of these gentlemen in order to establish Lalor's motives. A comparison of the evidence given before both committees suggests that personal pecuniary interest was the prime motive behind his unwillingness to pay tithes. He admitted to the Lords Committee, for instance, that the tithe composition was, in fact, 'beneficial', at least to men 'holding very small portions [of land] under ten acres (16.2 statute) or perhaps six (9.7) or seven (11.3) acres; but', he added, 'I have been speaking to several of those holding from six acres and upwards, who told me that they were injured by it'.[23] The tithe computation was, it seems, graded in favour of the small holder. Small occupiers were not, initially, against tithe at all — at least on economic grounds, as they did not have a say in its applotment. According to Lalor, it was decided on, in theory at least, by '25 of the largest occupiers, and . . . added to them £50 freeholders, and also magistrates possessing a certain quantity of property in the parish'. The committee pressed home its point: 'Did not that composition very seriously affect you, holding 500 acres of grassland?', they asked. 'It did', he replied, and followed this with an outburst against 'the vestries held for the assessment of church cess' which he opposed not only on legal and moral grounds, but also because he was, in his own words, 'one of the largest cess-payers in the parish'.[24]

Though Lalor's public campaign against tithe was articulated as a passive/moral crusade in the best interests of 'the people', it was clearly a class issue; for tithes, like vestries, were a church tax levied on *some*, not all, landholders.[25] In fact, the only popular (indeed, almost revolutionary) aspect of Lalor's anti-tithe doctrine was its designs on church lands. On the basis that, so far as he could learn, there were some 850 church dignitaries entitled to tithes who controlled a total of 714,735 acres of land,[26] Lalor argued that

> if the church lands were fairly and equitably disposed of by the State, it would make a much greater sum than would be necessary even to pay the same salaries that the clergy now receive; and if that was done, and any deficiency appeared, I do think the people would have no hesitation in paying the balance.

> What [he was asked] do you conceive would be a fair and equitable application of the church lands? — I conceive the equitable mode of managing them would be, that the Government should take them in hands, and set them to the best advantage to solvent and respectable tenants, and farm them in that way, and then the produce of them being taken by the State, should be in the first instance applied to the payment of the clergy; if there was any surplus, to put it to some other State purposes, and if there was any deficiency, to raise that in some other way, either as a land tax, or rather as a property tax.[27]

Whether 'solvent and respectable tenants' were to be found in a country in which land was 'taken as a matter of necessity, not as a speculation for making money' did not occur to Lalor. In addition, this proposed means of abolishing tithes, even if workable[28] (and it would require rather more detail than this witness has volunteered: e.g., what ratio of the gross produce would be allocated to the individual tenants as a reward for their enterprise) runs counter to his alternative assertion that 'it would be very unsafe and very improper for the Legislature ever to interfere in the private concerns of a gentleman in the disposal of his property'.[29]

While voicing these opinions (in 1832), 'Honest Pat' Lalor[30] was vigorously campaigning for parliament against a man who would later be a prime target for Fintan's veiled attacks on the aristocracy — the powerful local aristocrat, Sir Charles Henry Coote. Mr Lalor topped the poll with 772 votes, and 'Honest' Peter Gale, his running-mate, narrowly lost the second seat to Coote by a mere eleven votes.[31] However, the contest proved costly in more than one respect for both sides. Coote was attacked by a mob immediately following the official returns, and two people were killed and several wounded when the cavalry went to his aid. In a separate incident, a Mr Roe of Borris-in-Ossory, one of Coote's supporters, was also attacked though he killed his assailant in self-defence. And a similar attack in Maryborough on the same evening brought the death toll to four; undoubtedly a high price to pay for a 'popular' victory. Lalor, too, came under attack though his assailants, fortunately, used less violent weapons. The *Leinster Express* proved less than sparing in its abuse of his position and his supporters, claiming that he was a tyrant to his tenants — a claim later repeated by William Conner — and that he was secretly a tithe proctor. Nor was that all. His opponents attempted to unseat him on petition, and though this manoeuvre eventually proved unsuccessful, it nonetheless inflated his total election expenses to £5,000.[32]

All the major elements of Fintan's career were, thus, present in his father's rise to prominence in the early 1830s. The penchant for legal niceties, the veiled attack on ascendancy property, the personalist politics of a family feud, and even the confusing *laissez faire* principles used to explicate the role of government, were later employed (albeit in a more radical fashion) by Fintan. The parallels in their respective theories are, therefore, all the more remarkable given the often strained nature of their relationship throughout Fintan's life.

Born on 10 March 1807, Fintan injured his spine in infancy (apparently he was dropped by his nurse) and was a hunchback for the rest of his life. Though lively enough as a child, he attended none of the local schools. Possibly to shelter him from the rough-and-tumble, or from the cruelty of childish nicknames, he received private tuition at home until the age of seventeen. In February 1825, mid-way through the academic year, he was admitted to Carlow College where he studied for one year. His physical deformity, however, meant that dancing classes, physical training and sports were not part of his curriculum. In addition, poor health often confined him to his bed and obliged him to miss classes in Chemistry, Law, and the Classics.[33] Although there was a six week break during the summer, he stayed on in Carlow College for all but two of those and returned to his studies when the academic year resumed on the 8th of August. But, the ensuing winter proved too hard for him, and in February 1826, after only one (calendar) year of formal schooling, he returned to Tinakill.

Very little is known of his subsequent activities. Oral tradition has it that he became an apprentice to Dr John Jacob in the County Hospital at Maryborough and studied for the entrance examinations to the Royal College of Surgeons.[34] Dr Jacob's practice was taken over by his son in 1827 and, as a consequence of a difference of opinion, Lalor allegedly quit his employment, sold his horse and travelled to France. Though a rival story has it that he threw up his apprenticeship because of a hopeless love affair,[35] the allure of a French connection proved too tempting for Miss Fogarty:

> His life abroad was a restless one [she wrote in 1918]. He was covetous of experience, action, adventure. The parts of France whose associations attracted him, he explored, quiety with something of a devotee's ardour. Around the capital especially he found countless footprints which he followed with passionate interest, living the crowded days and months of 1789 over again.[36]

This spectral *persona* is presented as fact despite Miss Fogarty's admission that: 'No detailed information as to the friends he made . . . is obtainable'. She claims that this is due to the fact that 'all correspondence, diaries, and such-like documentary evidence' was impounded by the police during the suppression of the *Felon*.[37] In view of Lalor's penchant for hoarding letters it seems unlikely that any were written by or to him at this time. The lack of documentary evidence would, in fact, seem to imply that he was at home in the period from 1827 to 1831 — a situation which, if true, would render it absurd for members of his family to write him, or he them.[38] At any rate, Lalor was definitely in Tinakill in 1831 when the tithe agitation was beginning. In view of his later theories of agrarian issues, it may seem surprising that he did not publicly support his father (as the other sons did) at the hustings, despite the fact that Patrick Lalor was the foremost local agitator against tithes and was as a consequence returned as a Member of Parliament for the county from 1832 to 1835.[39] Fintan's absence may have been due to paternal concern for his health or, uncharitable as it may seem, to embarrassment for his physical deformities. Or it may be that Fintan had already joined the entourage of William Conner, an agrarian radical whose views on the land question were not confined to tithe commutation. Both men were of a like abrasive temperament, and no doubt Conner's legal training and his concern for those on the lower rungs of the rural social ladder struck a responsive chord in Fintan, whose one year of formal schooling had provided a course in 'Political Economy, the Elements of Law in General and in particular the Laws and Constitutions of this Country'.[40] Conner's arguments, therefore, with their appeal to law and their concern for economic principles[41] were of a kind which Lalor could appreciate. This is not to suggest that he fell so completely under Conner's sway that he uncritically accepted everything the Master said or wrote. In many respects this period is best seen as a further episode in Lalor's education, voluntarily 'apprenticing' himself to Conner in order to improve his understanding of 'applied' law and economics.

How long this apprenticeship lasted is not certain, though by November 1840 he had progressed sufficiently to set up in business, in a modest way, for himself. At his suggestion the local Temperance Society in Raheen changed its name to the *Shamrock Friendly Society* and had, as one of its principal aims, the policy of giving free legal advice to the poor.[42] Lalor was secretary to the Society. Subsequently, in March 1842, Conner was imprisoned for a seditious public address delivered in Mountmellick, as a result of which his ideas, and he himself, became a political liability and an embarrassment. As a result, he was drummed out of the Repeal Association. By that time, however, Lalor had left the Kildareman's entourage. Within five years it would be a source of considerable irritation to him that he had ever had anything to do with William Conner of Inch.

(ii) PUBLIC LIFE

'Since the present contest began it is eighteen years',[43] Lalor asserted in 1848. The agitation with which he wished to be associated, therefore, had its origins in 1830 and was roughly co-terminous with the opening salvoes of the tithe war. However, superseded by concern with the Irish poor law, and swamped by the emerging Loyal National Repeal Association, the land problem was driven beyond the pale of acceptable political discussion after the tithe act of 1838. Without shelving the issue, Lalor accepted its demise as a popular and a party grievance and sought less orthodox ways of agitating. In 1843, at a time when his father was publicly proclaiming that once repeal had been secured there would be time and opportunity enough to implement Conner's recommendations regarding independent valuation and security of tenure,[44] Fintan was corresponding with the British Prime Minister, Sir Robert Peel. 'I have long seen and felt', he wrote,

> the absolute necessity which exists, that ALL agitation for political objects should entirely cease, before any improvement can be effected in the condition of the Irish people. I am most anxious that the present Repeal-movement should be speedily and safely suppressed — not imperfectly and for a period, but fully and for ever. To effect that object I wish to contribute whatever little aid it may be in my power to give.[45]

Peel was impressed and sent the letter to the Home Secretary, Sir James Graham, and to Prince Albert. This was followed by a second letter which, though no longer extant, also evoked considerable interest.[46] Whether Pat Lalor knew of this correspondence or not is uncertain. At any rate, as a result of a long article which Fintan wrote on the subject of an Irish Agricultural Society,[47] the strains inherent in their relationship surfaced and in Janury 1844, at his father's insistence, Fintan left Tinakill. When the break came it seems to have been caused explicity by political differences. These, however, merely cloaked a wider and deeper divide in which the eldest son chafed under the yoke of paternal dependence. The death of Mrs Lalor in 1835, and of Joseph (the third son) at about the same time, may have been exacerbated by the fact that the family was breaking up, each individual member going out into his/her own life — William emigrating to America, Mary getting married[48] — whilst Fintan remained, a prisoner of his ill-health. This in itself would have been a source of considerable chagrin to him. In addition, his mother's death may have tended to aggravate the abrasive relationship with his father. From a domestic, 'psychological' point of view, Fintan was a natural rebel. Hamstrung by his lack of independence, trapped by his physical deformity, he seemed fated to remain always under his father's watchful eye.

From Tinakill, Fintan went to Dublin where, during his first winter away from home, his health broke. Though his siblings appealed to him to return home — especially as Jerome was preparing to emigrate to the United States; and despite the fact that his father, on hearing how bad he was, sent him money — Fintan nonetheless remained in 'exile'. When his health improved, he involved himself in a scheme to set up a bank providing loans at reasonable rates to the poor,[49] and travelled to Belfast to study a similar scheme under Fr Finn's direction. Finn advised him to drop the project. In June 1845 his health failed him once more and his condition remained critical throughout July. Improving slightly, he applied in September for the post of librarian and teacher at the Belfast Mechanics Institute, and secured some excellent references from, among others, Dr Robert Cane, the Mayor of Kilkenny.[50] However, the post was not vacated so he returned to Dublin and took lodgings in Trinity Street. His health deteriorated again and he was invalided throughout the winter. After a night of suffering in which he felt he was about to die, he decided that his only hope of convalescing lay in returning home. Too weak to travel on his own, his brother Thomas was sent to fetch him when he left Dublin for Tinakill in March 1846.

In the following January, already much improved, he wrote the letter to Duffy which marked his entry into the political arena. The fall of Sir Robert Peel's government in May 1846 and the Young Irelanders split with O'Connell soon afterwards, provided a fortuitous political *conjoncture* which favored Lalor's emergence. The former may have undermined his faith in the Conservative Party, whilst the latter suited his personal dislike of O'Connellite politics.[51] In addition, the famine may have been an important factor 'in driving him to take up the pen once more on behalf of the tenant farmers'.[52] There was, however, a more obvious auxiliary factor: his silence during the years of 'exile', was more than likely due to his inability to find his feet in a world which had little in the way of suitable, remunerative employment to offer a young man who was a hunchback and suffered from asthma and tuberculosis. Despite the fact that his father had helped to finance his 'exile', it was only on his return to the relative stability of the Tinakill household that Fintan once more found the conditions needed in order to write. Freed from the drudgery of day-to-day independence he once more set about propagating his ideas.

'I invited him', wrote Duffy, 'to state his opinions in the *Nation*, instead of committing them to my private ear; and he wrote three letters in quick succession, which were marvels of passionate persuasive rhetoric'.[53] However, even the passion of 'this new tribune of the people'[54] was not persuasive enough to force the Irish Confederation to formulate a realistic policy to deal as a movement with the catastrophe of famine. In his heated correspondence with Duffy, Mitchel, Doheny and D'Arcy McGee (in which he energetically lobbied for support) Lalor proposed that a rent-strike by the smaller tenants should be organised, and officially supported by the Confederation. This would not only be a realistic reaction to the social and economic dislocation caused by the famine but would, in addition, provide the only lever by which popular support could be weaned away from the Repeal Association and put at the disposal of the Confederation. The reaction to this policy was immediate and intense. Duffy had previously written in reply to Lalor's first letter:

> I can well fancy you bringing an untrained Titanic force into our counsels that would flutter the conventionalities of certain trim and curled gentlemen — but for me I can sincerely assure you that I will be heartily glad to see you amongst us, and, if you allow me, will move you at once to our council.[55]

Duffy baulked, however, once the full ramifications of Lalor's programme had sunk in. In March the Confederation formed a committee which delegated to Smith O'Brien the task of formulating official Confederation policy.[56] The resulting pamphlet on *Reproductive Employment* pleased no one. Mitchel was emphatic: 'certainly we do not like *this* Report as an exposition of Confederate policy'. Duffy was more diplomatic: 'Your report would make a useful lecture'.[57] Both of them provided alternatives. Duffy, who contended that 'nowhere has a popular movement succeeded that did not exhaust the resources of the Constitution first'[58] now proposed that the Confederation should 'seize upon all the institutions which still remain to the country — the corporations, grand juries, boards of guardians, town commissioners, and the representatives of Ireland in the Imperial Parliament'.[59] It was Smith O'Brien's non-policy which had forced Duffy's hand; the latter's response which brought Mitchel into the open with his recommendation of a strike against poor rate; and it was Lalor's published letters in *The Nation* and private letters to members of the Confederation which had begun the series. The result was four policies in search of a movement. In the event, they all failed.

Disappointed with the Confederation's response Lalor decided to go it alone, and he organised a meeting of tenants at Holycross, County Tipperary in September 1847. The attempt to create a Tenants' Association was not novel. Lalor was, at the time, corresponding with William Trenwith who was secretary of a similar association in Cork.[60] On the day of the Holycross meeting, however, Lalor came under fire not only from P.B. Ryan — whose agitation in the area, and whose ties with Trenwith, preceded Lalor's — but also from William Conner of Inch. In the course of a heated exchange between Fintan and Conner the platform collapsed, the crowd dispersed after a show of hands in favour of the proposed Association, and Conner harangued their backs with his own brand of peasant politics whilst his ex-pupil was carried shoulder-high to the nearest pub![61]

In the wake of this fiasco, the Tenant Association of Tipperary was quickly and quietly interred and the proposed rent strike never materialised. Lalor, understandably, 'retired from interference with public affairs quite disheartened'.[62] Yet his failure here is instructive, as it provided the impetus for his later involvement in the *Felon*, founded after Mitchel had been transported for his militant articles in *The United Irishman*. That journal had been founded by Mitchel when it became clear to him, and to Duffy, that their policies were now diametrically opposed. Whereas the latter remained a strict constitutionalist, Mitchel abandoned his earlier policy of a strike against poor-rate in favour of militant resistance to the Crown forces in Ireland. Martial rhetoric was not new to Irish politics. Even O'Connell had been known to use it from time to time. In the course of 1848, Lalor too became enamoured with the politics of the pike and the martial rhetoric which it entailed. However, the reasons for his involvement are suspect, not least because of the stern refusal with which he had greeted Mitchel's invitation to contribute to *The United Irishman*. This initial rebuff must seem all the more puzzling given Lalor's subsequent willingness to involve himself in founding and co-editing John Martin's *Irish Felon*. Established as 'a journal intended to fill the place and take up the mission of *The United Irishman*'[63] the *Felon* ran for five issues, and Fintan contributed no less than seven articles, all of which could legitimately claim to be 'following' this editorial line. However, whilst his final contributions were stridently militant in tone if not in content, his earlier letters were deliberate, cogently argued essays on land and related issues.

The problem, therefore, is this: if Lalor *was* a militant nationalist in the pages of the *Felon*, why the unwillingness to involve himself in Mitchel's paper at a time when both men had long since ceased to contribute to

The Nation? And, why the sudden seeming conversion after Mitchel's transportation? The truth of the matter appears to be that Mitchel's scheme of a strike against poor-rate was an unacknowledged adaptation of Fintan's original rent-strike policy and was, in fact, a major factor in alienating possible sources of support for Lalor's ideas. He could *not* involve himself as a contributor to *The United Irishman* for, clearly, such a move would only further undermine his position by giving the impression that he shared Mitchel's ideas. In fact, the reverse would seem to have been the case. As early as February 1847, when one of Fintan's early letters was being circulated among the members of the Confederation, Mitchel wrote to him 'stating that on perusal and consideration of its contents, he had fully adopted my views, and that he meant to act on them so soon as occasion should fit and serve'.[64] That he did not do so does not invalidate Lalor's claim that 'between . . . Mitchel and myself there was from the first an *almost* perfect agreement'. Mitchel concurs. In August 1847, when Lalor was 'prosecuting an agitation amongst the farmers of Tipperary', Mitchel declared to Smith O'Brien that, on 'the ultimate settlement of the tenure question . . . my doctrine is nearly identical with Lalor's'. A month later, hoping to prod O'Brien and the Confederation into a more forceful public stance on the land question, he added:

a fair, or a tolerably fair, scheme of tenant right . . . will take the people out of the hands of Lalor and all revolutionists. But the time has nearly come when affairs must take a decisive turn, either in one way or the other. I sincerely hope it will be in the moderate direction.[65]

Though Mitchel's moderation gave way shortly thereafter to full-blown militarism, and some others (including Lalor) followed suit, the available evidence suggests that Fintan was not at heart a physical-force man. He might militantly rebel, but he preferred peaceful revolution. He might support nationalism, but he dreamed of democracy. So, when John Martin invited him to help in establishing the *Felon* he acceded and, by degrees, adopted the sort of militant journalism which had made *The United Irishman* a success. This after all was the publicly proclaimed editorial line; for the *Felon* had been founded as a self-conscious successor to *The United Irishman*. It does not necessarily follow, however, that Lalor was a nationalist in the militant Mitchelite mould simply because he wrote some militant articles for a Mitchelite journal. In fact, it might more feasibly be argued that, given his training as an attorney, Mitchel was a 'Lalorite' — one of those with a basic understanding of legal matters (D'Arcy McGee was another) who were attracted to Fintan's ideas because of their solid foundation in legal principles. As Mitchel had apparently appropriated *his* basic tenets, Fintan may have felt justified in plagiarising the Mitchelite pose in the *Felon*.

One further point may help to elucidate the motives behind Lalor's apparent change of heart. When invited to contribute to the *Felon* he tempered his obvious enthusiasm with the suggestion that the paper should be managed as a joint-stock enterprise, having 'four or five competent editors . . . one at least of [whom] should be an English Chartist of known talent and honesty'.[66] In itself, such a proposal was not alarming. In early 1848 Confederate and Repeal organisations began to merge with Chartist clubs and more than one man would have fitted Lalor's bill. Two at least were personally acquainted with him: J.D. Balfe, a Liverpool Chartist who had settled in Dublin early in 1847 was vice-president of that 'regular *sans-culottish* looking conventicle',[67] the St Patrick's Club (of which Lalor was president); and B.T. Treanor, with whom he had corresponded and who founded a Felon Club in Stanleybridge in England.[68] Either of these could have filled the post at a time when the 'hot-headed Irish landowner'[69] Feargus O'Connor (who supported Irish Repealers)[70] was emerging as the most prominent and uncompromising propagandist of the Chartist cause and the Chartist Land Plan.[71] Given Lalor's concern for Irish agrarian issues and his hatred of repeal, what he may have envisaged, therefore, was a coup of sorts: viz, to wean O'Connor's support away from repeal and establish its similarities with the kind of movement he personally preferred. Chartists had supported Mitchel's militant line; it remained to be seen whether they would support Lalor's.[72]

In mid-July 1848, before any response to these tentative feelers for support could emerge, the *Felon* offices were visited by the police. Lalor escaped unscathed at a time when, *habeas corpus* having been suspended, all the major propagandists went in fear for their continued liberty. Wanted for his part in the *Felon,* and in particular to help identify authors and articles in that journal for the trial of John Martin,[73] Lalor was finally arrested at Ballyhane, near Nenagh, prior to the outbreak of hostilities in the Widow MacCormack's cabbage patch. He was first lodged in the local gaol before being transferred to Newgate Prison in Dublin, where he remained incarcerated until released because of ill-health in November 1848. Despite the futile gestures of militancy which he made when on the run in Tipperary[74] there is very little evidence of any activity by Lalor at this juncture that could, realistically, be termed 'revolutionary'. His sole contribution to the 1848 fiasco seems to have been the renewed impetus which his *Felon* articles gave to Duffy's growing paranoia. 'There will be an outburst sooner or later, be sure of that', Duffy had written to Smith O'Brien

> But unless you provide against it, it will be a mere democratic one . . . [and] you and I will meet on a Jacobin scaffold, ordered for execution as enemies of some new Marat or Robespierre, Mr James Lalor or Mr Somebody else [i.e., Mitchel].[75]

This extraordinary letter, had he but been aware of it, would undoubtedly have convinced Fintan of the futility of seeking Duffy's aid in any future projects. As it happened he was none the wiser when, immediately after his release, he set about trying to establish another journal as a successor to the *Felon*, and (innocently) wrote to the still incarcerated Duffy:

> I am urged by several parties, of different shades of green, to join them in a new movement. I can no longer delay giving an answer, one way or the other, and acting accordingly. I must step out or stand by. There is a very general fermentation going on below surface. The movement everywhere is running spontaneously into secret organisation, and I think *natural tendency* ought to be aided not interfered with. A new journal, conducting itself with *prudence* and *propriety,* would be indispensable to any new movement. Now, on this matter . . . We ought to have but one journal, that is clear, and clear, too, that you should be at the head of it . . . Is there anything to hinder you from being proprietor of a paper while there, or from writing its articles? I can see nothing — nothing at least that could not be got over. You could not superintend details, but you could write the more, *there* would be all the difference.[76]

Duffy, understandably, had no interest in this scheme and declared he 'had no confidence in conspiracy'.[77] Later attempts to found a journal proved equally barren. In the secret clubs, which Lalor had helped to establish in 1849, the internal political squabbles, especially between himself and Joseph Brennan (editor of the *Irishman*), were fought on the lines of a newspaper war. Brennan, obviously, had no wish to compete with any new journal which Lalor might establish. He, therefore, attempted to oust his would-be competitor from positions of power in the clubs. When Lalor visited Fr John Kenyon in the early summer of '49, Brennan saw his chance and promptly 'took over leadership in the city'.[78] In the event, Lalor lost not only the chance to found his own paper (a project for which he was attempting to raise public subscriptions throughout the countryside during his visit to Kenyon), but also his control of policy in the clubs. A simultaneous uprising was planned for September in counties Cork,

Limerick, Clare, Kilkenny, Tipperary and Waterford. In the event, there was but a minor skirmish at Cappoquin, and ominous inactivity everywhere else. Lalor apparently 'lay out all night waiting to lead an attack on Cashel barracks but was joined by a force which he considered totally inadequate'.[79] In fact, he had been joined by 'some hundred or hundred and fifty men, and not badly armed', and was to have teamed up with John O'Leary who had been put in charge of some 'forty or fifty . . . mostly armed' men from the same area. In view of the fact that a similar number (i.e., 200) had been involved in the abortive attack on Cappoquin barracks it might seem that Lalor and O'Leary were right to dismiss their recruits as numerically inadequate for the job. However, two points invalidate this. First, O'Leary dismissed his recruits *before* he had rendezvoused with Lalor,[80] and the latter — despite having at his disposal a large force of volunteers — was conspicuously immobile all night. Despite his strident verbal nationalism, therefore, it seems clear that Lalor was *not* a physical force activist. He could adopt the pose, but he could not die for or by it. This is not to assert that he was an unmitigated coward. His quandary was shared by many in the late 1840s. Having been hounded into the open by the backlog of their own martial rhetoric they sensed its futility once in the field. It was all very well to dream of leading Irishmen to glory and freedom, but as Smith O'Brien had learned to his acute embarrassment, where the rank-and-file are thin on the ground it is easier to follow than to lead.

Fintan returned to Dublin, depressed by the fiasco which he had left behind in Tipperary. He toyed with the idea of writing for *The Nation*, but — once his spirits had lifted a little — decided instead to revive his plan to start his own paper. The scheme never reached fruition. His health, damaged no doubt by his all-night vigil in a Tipperary ditch, failed him once more and he died on December 27, 1849.

(iii) CONCLUSIONS

Lalor's character and career were shaped by nothing so much as his health, particularly his physical deformity. It not only kept him from formal schooling, but also, it seems, severely limited his employability. When, in 1847, he entered the public political arena it was a source of considerable chagrin to him that his ideas were deemed forceful and rigorously logical by everyone — until they met him. Doheny, who helped him to organise the Holycross meeting, wrote to Duffy: 'I could not be persuaded that I had before me, in the poor, distorted, ill-favoured hunch-backed little creature, the bold propounder of the singular doctrines in the *Nation* letters.'[81] Surprised, and perhaps even repelled to some extent, by Lalor's physical features, those who knew him in these years later wrote of him in terms that made it clear that such factors weighed more heavily with them than did his intellectual abilities. According to O'Leary:

While Lalor was at bottom a good, if not a good-natured, man his nature, as is but too often the case with men labouring under his peculiar physical deformity . . ., had contracted a sort of moral twist. He was, if not malignant in the English sense, certainly what the French call *malin.* His humour was sometimes horribly sardonic.[82]

For John Savage also, physical factors loomed large, though he intimates that they had a positive effect on Lalor's prose style:

Of a deformed person, ungainly action, comparatively blind and deaf, soured in temper, splenetic, bitter and self-opinionated, he was one of the most powerful political writers that ever took pen in hand. His arguments were as logical as his conclusions were fierce; his denunciations as bitter as they were eloquent, and his style as pure as his indignation was savage. The more ferocious his intentions, the better was his English; and *never being in an amiable mood*, his manner, consequently, was never faulty.[83]

For Duffy, however, the connection between Lalor's health and writings was of a negative sort. Not being enamoured with Lalor's ideas he undermined them by evaluating them in terms of Fintan's unfortunate disability:

Having never known the invaluable discipline of rivals and competitors to reduce his plans to practical dimensions, he nourished an indomitable intellectual pride in his work which was probably aggravated by the necessity a deformed man feels to insist upon his individuality. Had he been six feet high, had his sane and vigorous intellect been lodged in a sane and vigorous body, had his *amour-propre*, which was irritated by opposition and unreasonable contempt, been soothed by sympathy and success, he might have rivalled Tone or Owen O'Neill.[84]

Whether possessing 'a sane and vigorous body' or not, it is hard to imagine *anyone* whose *amour-propre* could possibly fail to have been 'irritated by . . . unreasonable contempt'. In fact there is nothing in Duffy's account which would lead us to believe that he, at any rate, was capable of sympathising with Lalor's disability. At the mercy of such reactions, therefore, it is hardly surprising that Fintan was irritated and annoyed by those contemporaries who proved more willing to judge the book by its cover than by its contents. In addition, given the manner in which his original proposals were juggled (and eventually dropped) by the Irish Confederation in the summer of 1847, and in which his position and influence in the secret societies were undermined two years later by Brennan, Lalor had just grounds for being suspicious of his fellow workers — though, they imply that he was suspicious by nature, or as a result of his physical deformity.

Not so important, perhaps, as his ill-health, Lalor's social background was nonetheless a vital factor in shaping his outlook. As the son of a prosperous 'gentleman farmer' there is little in his life or career that would validate the contention that:

No one understood better than Lalor the awful condition of the peasantry; no writer of the period felt it more personally, more acutely. The purest, and most highly gifted, people on the face of the earth held up as objects of public alms by those whose ingenuity and legislative foresight had brought about their destruction! Infuriated, Lalor spoke out — *spoke as one of them* . . . he had the preliminary advantage (over Davis and Mitchel) of being a democrat by birth, not by conviction. He knew his peasantry; he knew his "landed gentry" and although he may have overestimated the military prowess of the former, he never suffered from any illusions about the latter.[85]

As the son of a middleman who controlled one thousand statute acres, Fintan Lalor could not, under any circumstances, be described as a peasant. Whilst he may have understood their plight better than, say, Davis or Duffy, it would nevertheless be very wide of the mark indeed to claim that he 'spoke as one of them'. Insofar as he wrote and acted as a self-appointed spokesman for the small-holders, his view of their plight, his proposals for the amelioration of their lot and his reasons for seeking to champion their cause are open to question. This is not to suggest that, consciously or otherwise, he acted purely out of personal or class interests. However, the motives for his concern need to be examined rather more critically and carefully than has been the case to date. To explain his position by describing him as a Nationalist or as a Socialist is insufficient as this merely changes the nature of the question. Why, for instance, did he become a Nationalist or a Socialist and, more specifically, why was he so concerned with the plight of the small-holders as opposed, say, to the plight — in many respects much worse — of the agricultural labourers?

Indeed, the justification for using ideological tags in describing or interpreting Lalor's career is highly suspect. When writing to Sir Robert Peel in 1843 he proclaimed:

I was, myself, at one time something *more* than a mere Repealer, in private feeling — but Mr O'Connell, his *agitators,* and his series of wretched agitations, first *disgusted* me into a conservative in point of *feeling*, and reflection and experience have convicted me into one in point of *principle*.[86]

Three years later he used the same tone and content to declare to Duffy: 'I was a Repealer in private feeling at one time, for I hardly know that I can say that I am one now, having almost taken a hatred and disgust to this my own country and countrymen.'[87] Just as earlier he had declared himself a Conservative to Peel, so now he professed himself a seceder to Duffy, and with equal success. In fact, his theories were plastic constructs, malleable enough to be moulded (as Lalor did mould them) to cover *all* of the many factions involved in Irish politics in this period.

In the course of the heated debate on the relative demerits of Physical and Moral force which had revealed the gulf which yawned between Repeal and Young Ireland, O'Connell had defined himself as an 'Old Irelander' in obvious contrast to Davis' movement. In order to paper over these early cracks, Smith O'Brien had jocularly suggested that he, at any rate, preferred 'Middle-Aged Ireland', and Richard O'Gorman completed the generations and the debate when he aptly and succinctly dubbed the politics of the pike as 'Infant Ireland'.[88] By 1847/48, however, the joke was seen to have miscarried when all of these positions were taken up, at various times and with varying degrees of success, by those involved in the series of splits which wracked Irish politics in the period. Lalor was aware of these differences of outlook and approach and, subsequent to his personal failure at Holycross, involved himself in both Smith O'Brien's and Mitchel's militant adventures in 1848/49.

The impression one gets from Lalor's career, however, is that he preferred the role of ideologue to that of activist; and, specifically, that the prospect of a guaranteed readership for his projected paper was the prime motive for his involvement in the affairs of the secret societies of 1849. Not that he wished to wield a gun or a pike but that he wished to wield a pen and continue to propagate his ideas. It is largely on the basis of his activities in 1848/49 that Lalor is interpreted as Nationalist or a Republican, and there is no shortage of quotable material from his writing which would seem to validate the contention. However, the reasons adduced to explain his intellectual pilgrimage from Conservatism in 1843 to Republican Nationalism in 1849 are not tenable and, in fact, founder specifically on the rock of his social/agrarian theories. As he himself put it in his letter to Peel:

I have been *driven* into the conviction, more strongly confirmed by every day's experience, that it is only to a Conservative Government, to her landed proprietors, and to *peace* that this country can look for any improvements in her social condition.[89]

Obviously, his concern for Ireland's 'social condition' is more sincerely felt that his professed Conservatism. In fact, what patently emerges from even the most cursory consideration of Lalor's brief career, is the essentially chameleonic nature of his political persuasions. His core ideas were fully developed by the early 'forties and did not undergo any fundamental change thereafter.[90] By slightly reworking his letters and papers he could suit them to fit different readers (Peel, Duffy) and changed circumstances. Lalor, in fact, spent the best part of his time and energies hawking his ideas about from post to pillar in the (vain) hope that some individual, club, or party would sponsor and help to realise them. In the process, he began and ended with two brief flirtations with English parties: Peel's Conservatives in 1843, and O'Connor's Chartists five years later. In the meantime, aware of the rifts in Young Ireland, he followed its fortunes and adapted his theories to fit the changed circumstances, running with Smith O'Brien's 'Middle-Aged Ireland' in '48 and with a Mitchelite 'Infant Ireland' organisation in '49. He, in fact, embraced, at one time or other, however briefly, practically every available political credo of the decade. Therefore, it is more feasible to view his career, not as an intellectual journey towards his final position (O'Neill's interpretation), but as a search for political sponsorship of certain ideas which remained always central for him. However, the precise nature of these ideas is by no means easy to discern. Given their foundation in legal principles, the examination and explication of his theories can best begin with an account and assessment of his appeal to law.

2

Lalor's Appeal to Law

(i) REFORM AND REACTION

English radical politics and the drift towards reform — though temporarily stifled by the wholly predictable, ultra-conservative backlash during the years of revolution and war — revived almost immediately after the defeat of Napoleon's armies in 1815. Within five years of the reactionary triumph the domestic reforming drift had become a flood. Fed by the post-war economic depression, by the social disruption consequent on rapid industrialisation and urbanisation, and by the idealised martyrology of its initial defeats (the Spa Fields Riot, 1816; the 'Peterloo Massacre', 1819; the repressive Six Acts, 1819) the movement for reform dominated English politics in the early nineteenth century and, subsequently, gave its name to the age.[1]

English reformism was dominated by the drive for political change, and characterised by the — often tortuous — pursuit of class identity and consciousness. Paradoxically, though the necessity for reform was a shared conviction, and hence a unifying factor, the question of identity tended to fragment and divide the movement. 'Middle-class' reformism may have been largely placated by the 1832 Reform Act, but 'working-class' discontent with the new arrangement gave rise to Chartism and the coherent beginnings of theoretical socialism.

Irish reformism (dominated by O'Connell's Emancipation and Repeal movements) shared both the drive for fundamental political change and the quest for identity, though the latter was largely developed and articulated by Thomas Davis and centered on nationality rather than class. Because these movements were not only contemporaneous but parallel,

Irish reformers were apt to use the terminology of their English counterparts. Despite — or, perhaps, because of — this shared vocabulary, Irish reformers became more conscious of the differences between their own largely agricultural and 'traditional' society and an increasingly industrial and urban England. Diverging economies exacerbated tensions within the Union, and greatly facilitated the development of modern Irish nationalism. Diverging social conditions, a consequence of diverging economies, diminished English perceptions of Irish grievances and enabled Irish nationalists the more easily to point out what was distinctive about Ireland, and how and why she differed from England.

Conservatives in both countries, in opposing such reform movements, were apt to portray them as demonically-inspired conspiracies which aimed to subvert 'the laws, constitution and government and every existing establishment, civil or ecclesiastical, *both* in Great Britain and Ireland'.[2] Conservatism, therefore, came to be seen as a largely reactionary, and often hysterical, defence of the *status quo*. Given the entrenched legal nature of aristocratic rights and privileges, jurists inevitably emerged as the most important defenders and legitimists of Conservatism, and William Blackstone's *Commentaries on the laws of England*[3] became their bulwark and bible against the growing ranks of reformers. Indeed, the task of defending the (unwritten) constitution and the (uncodified) law may not have been made appreciably easier for them, as the *Commentaries* are full of those mildewed legal fictions and intricacies so beloved of lawyers and jurists. Blackstone, for example, typically argues in the following manner: in England, as perhaps nowhere else, 'political or civil liberty is the very end and scope of the constitution'. However, 'this liberty, rightly understood, consists in the power of doing what the law permits'. Thus, good law is defined as that which best preserves individual liberty, and individual liberty is defined as that which is permitted by the law![4] Such anomalies, so proudly presented as coherent and reasoned arguments by the foremost jurist of the day, were trifling considerations for one who could write:

> Of a constitution, so wisely contrived, so strongly raised, and so highly finished, it is hard to speak with that praise which is justly and severely its due: – the thorough and attentive contemplation of it will furnish its best panegyric.
> It hath been the endeavour of these commentaries . . . to demonstrate [its] elegant proportions . . . We have taken the occasion to admire . . . the noble monuments of ancient simplicity, and the more curious refinements of modern art. Nor have its faults been concealed from view; for faults it has, lest we should be tempted to think

it of more than human structure; defects, chiefly arising from the decays of time, or the rage of unskilful improvements in later ages (sic). To sustain, to repair, to beautify this noble pile, is a charge intrusted principally to the nobility, and such gentlemen of the Kingdom as are delegated by their country to parliament. The protection of the *Liberty of Britain* is a duty which they owe to themselves, who enjoy it; to their ancestors, who transmitted it down; and to their posterity, who will claim at their hands this, the best birthright, and the noblest inheritance of mankind.[5]

These, as Professor Dicey rightly remarks, are the sentiments 'not of an individual but of an era'[6] — an era, moreover, of profound confidence in English institutions. For, from the 'studied optimism of Blackstone' and its sequel 'the legislative timidity of Lord Eldon', there issued that 'pride in the English constitution, and intense satisfaction with things as they were'[7] which provided the self-assured, reactionary rocks on which so many reforming zealots came to grief.

However, though the matchless constitution so beloved of Eldon and Wellington was never seriously in jeopardy in England, (so long, that is, as it admitted of piecemeal reforms in order to bring it into line with changed social and economic conditions), the same was not true in Ireland, where the Act of Union of 1800 guaranteed the protection and preservation of ascendancy domination 'forever'.[8] The whig constitution of the 1680s was, thereby, being extended to Ireland at the very moment when it was most vulnerable in England. Inevitably, therefore, the Act of Union provided 'the matrix of modern Irish history',[9] and attitudes to law (including the recourse to 'illegal' means) were to play a vital part in the successive attempts to repeal this increasingly anachronistic statute. As Professor MacDonagh could put it:

The Act of Union possessed for many the solemnity of fundamental law, far beyond the pretensions of ordinary legislation. With the finality of a vast constitutional rearrangement, it fenced in the range of the politically possible in the nineteenth century.[10]

Despite its alleged finality, however, the 'Act of miscalculations' was not totally irreversible. Far from being an impervious and immovable stumbling-block, it was to provide a (dangerously?) convenient focus for Irish discontent during the age of reform and beyond. In fact, its seeming impervious finality may have been due in large measure to O'Connell's constitutionalist respect for the law and its institutions — a respect not often matched by other reforming zealots on either side of the Irish Sea. Given the man, his barrister's training, and his horror of political violence, it is perhaps not surprising that under his guidance Irish discontent took the form of a peaceful constitutional agitation; nor that lawyers accounted for 13 of the 51 O'Connellite M.P.s elected to Westminster in the early nineteenth century.[11] In fact, his much quoted boast that he could 'drive a coach-and-four through any Act of Parliament' was less an indictment of the woeful state of statutory law than a succinct summation of his preferred means of redress. However, adroit horsemanship alone would not of itself win repeal or assuage the angry doubts of those who, like James Fintan Lalor, despised O'Connell's nepotistic politics and believed repeal to be 'a leaky collier smack, with a craven crew to man her and a sworn dastard and forsworn traitor at the helm'.[12]

(ii) LALOR'S VIEW OF LAW

Lalor's disdain for both O'Connell and repeal was matched only by his vitriolic hatred of the Irish aristocracy, and it was against the tyranny of this 'class of eight thousand'[13] as owners of the land (and, hence, of the laws controlling Irish lives and liberties) that he brought the full brunt of his considerable talents to bear. At the root of his attack there lay an appeal to legal principles. However, whereas O'Connell's respect for the law ensured that he would always act constitutionally in seeking reforms, Lalor did not share the trained barrister's understanding of and sympathy for the profession or its institutions. As he put it in a letter to Duffy regarding the use of none but legal means: 'I speak, of course, in ignorance being no lawyer, thank God. But . . . any means and all means might be made illegal by Act of Parliament.'[14] Perhaps for this reason, he did not focus on an individual statute, as O'Connell was wont to do, but argued instead on the basis of what he regarded (taking Blackstone's *Commentaries* as his guide)[15] as fundamental, universally-valid legal principles. Thus, the interlocking, mutually-supportive theories of Natural Law and Social Contract together provide the underlying basis of his ideas.[16] In itself this is unremarkable; but, what *is* unusual is the manner in which he applies them to Irish conditions.

As Natural Law was viewed as a higher law, an ideal to which positive (or State) law ought to conform,[17] Lalor set out to prove that English law was at variance with its alleged theoretical roots. 'What founds and forms the rights of property in land?' he asked in the *Felon* in 1848.

> I have never read in the direction of that question. I have all my life been destitute of books. But from the first chapter of Blackstone's second book, the only page I ever

read on the subject, I know that jurists are unanimously agreed in considering 'first occupancy' to be the only true original foundation of the right of property and possession of land.[18]

However, 'first occupancy' is but a 'feeble and fictitious title . . . *invented by theorists*'[19] to cloak the fact that English conquest and colonisation were illegal contraventions of Natural Law. According to Blackstone 'when [a] mother country was overcharged with inhabitants' it tended to colonise adjacent regions and countries. However,

so long as it was confined to the stocking and cultivating of *desert uninhabited* countries, it kept strictly within the limits of the law of nature. But how far the seizing on countries already peopled, and driving out or massacring the innocent and defenceless natives, merely because they differed from their invaders in language, in religion, in customs, in government, or in colour: how far such conduct was consonant to nature, to reason, or to christianity, deserved well to be considered by those, who have rendered their names immortal by thus civilizing mankind.[20]

Though Blackstone walks up to the very maw of a declaration of the illegality of English imperialism before he perceives the implications of his argument and turns tail, Lalor is not so reticent in denouncing 'the robber rights' of an alien aristocracy. He argues that only in two modes 'that of conquest, or that of common agreement — have the distribution and settlement of the land of every country been made'.[21] Because only the second mode was valid, Lalor could correctly claim that his objective was 'to repeal the Conquest — not any part or portion but the whole entire conquest of seven hundred years'.[22] A year later, in the *Felon*, he reiterated that claim, and added:

I am reminded that there are few persons now who trouble themselves about the "conquest"; . . . I trouble myself as little as anyone does about [it] as taken abstractedly, as an affair that took place long ages ago. But the "conquest" is still in existence with all its laws, rights, claims, relations and results. The landlord holds his lands by right and title of conquest, and uses his powers as only a conqueror may. The tenant holds under the law of conquest — *vae victis*.[23]

However, titles based on conquest are illegitimate because they usurp the property rights of the aboriginal inhabitants, and subvert the original contract on which they are based. In addition, because laws established on this basis necessarily defend the rights of an alien minority, they cannot have the interests of the native people at heart. In the case of Ireland this has meant that the aristocratic domination of the polity has ensured the continuation of a venal approach to legislation and the administration of the law; and this, necessarily, has had wide and disastrous social and economic effects. It is not merely that the aristocracy 'who own your land will make your laws, and command your liberties and your lives', but that self-interest entails, in itself, that the privileged minority will inevitably 'fail to perform its duty and fulfill its office of providing for its people'.[24] The famine, in Lalor's eyes is the natural and inevitable outcome of the aristocratic departure from the constraints of *noblesse oblige*, the palpable consequence of the rift between positive law and natural law. As a result: 'Society stands dissolved', and therefore, 'a clear original right returns and reverts to the people — the right of establishing and entering into a new social arrangement', a new social contract.[25]

One of the most incisive, and enduring, criticisms of the Social Contract theory had been that it was *a priori* — that is, had no historical foundation whatsoever. For Lalor, the famine produced in Ireland a concrete, historical opportunity to apply the contract theory and make it work. Thus, in his first letter to *The Nation* he wrote:

> When society fails to perform its duty and fulfill its office of providing for its people; it must take another and more efficient form, or it must cease to exist. When its members begin to die out under destitution — when they begin to perish in thousands under famine and the effects of famine — when they begin to desert and fly from the land in hundreds of thousands under the force and fear of deadly famine — it is time to see it is God's will that society should stand dissolved, and assume another shape and action; and he works his will by human hands and natural agencies. This case has arisen even now in Ireland, and the effect has already followed in part. Society stands dissolved. In effect, as well as of right, it stands dissolved, and another requires to be constituted . . . A new adjustment is now to be formed, is to form and develop itself; a new social order to be arranged; a new people to be organised. . . . To any one who either looks to an immediate directing Providence, or trusts to a settled course of natural causes, it is clear that this island is about to take existence under a new tenure; or else that Nature has issued her decree — often issued heretofore against nations and races and ever for the same crime — that one other imbecile and cowardly people shall cease to exist, and no longer cumber the earth.[26]

As we shall see, 'society' versus 'the people' is, essentially, a class fight, a conflict between the landowning aristocracy and the tenantry. However, Lalor's immediate concern is to make it absolutely clear that the social contract which had characterised the *ancien régime* in Ireland has been swept away by the famine and that 'Nor heaven nor human nature will suffer it to be re-established'. He iterates again and again his conviction that 'a dissolution of the social system has taken place',[27] and continues:

The failure of the potato was the *immediate exciting* cause. Into the *predisposing* cause it is needless for the present to enquire. There was no outrise or revolt against it. It was not broken up by violence. It was borne for ages in beggarly patience, until it perished by the visitation of God in the order of nature.[28]

The predisposing causes were in fact the enormous (and, in Lalor's eyes, unbrigeable) rifts which existed, on racial, religious, social and economic grounds, between an alien aristocracy and a native people. For these reasons, and because they consistently failed to practice the duties of nobility, the aristocracy 'in some respects and in some degree . . . are considered chargeable with the calamitous crisis that has occurred'.[29] Their position is, at root, an un-natural one, because, as Lalor put it in his open letter to them in *The Nation:*

While from Ireland you take rank and revenue, blood and birth and name — everything that makes home, and binds to country — yet you look not to her, but to another land, for home and country; . . . you desert and disown, if not hate her old native people; . . . in England are your hearts and hopes, and . . . all your household gods are English . . . You have probably begun to find out that if your feelings are English, yet your fortunes are Irish; that Ireland's peril is perilous to yourselves; that in renouncing your country and adopting another, you renounce and revolt from the laws of nature.[30]

Their hold on Irish lands, their social and economic pre-eminence, their 'rights of ownership' and 'power of position', are criminal because they are un-natural anomalies. As a 'foreign garrison' which has refused to become a 'national guard', which by right of conquest has been given title of tenure to Irish lands, which 'ought of right to be where [it has] never chosen to be — at the head of this people';[31] for all these reasons the aristocrats *in* Ireland

form no class of the Irish people, or of any other people. Strangers they are in this land they call theirs — strangers here and strangers everywhere, owning no country and owned by none; rejecting Ireland, and rejected by England; tyrants to this island and slaves to another; here they stand hating and hated — their hand ever against us, as ours against them, an outcast and ruffianly hoarde, alone in the world, and alone in its history, a class by themselves.[32]

In assailing the pomp, power and position of this déclassé band of unwanted mavericks, Lalor forwards a double-stranded theory of sovereignty. At the international level, he asserts, individual countries are sovereign with respect to each other; and at the national level, internal sovereignty is based on the will of the people.

On the basis of the first principle Lalor claims that Ireland — despite conquest, partial colonisation, and a unilaterally imposed Union — retains its *de jure* sovereignty in its relations with England. But, *de facto,* Irishmen are slaves and Ireland a colony governed by a parliament which 'will NEVER, in form of law, repeal the Act of Union', and restore Irish independence, '*Never*, while the sun sits in heaven and the laws of nature are in action'.[33] Therefore the problem facing Irishmen is that of *convincing* Westminster that it has no moral or legal right to govern in Ireland. Lalor's preferred means of doing this would be to select 'one particular law to take [a] stand on, trample down, and nullify . . . one the abrogation of which would be an abrogation of sovereignty'.[34] Because he could discover no such law, he based his case on a principle of natural law which was 'beyond dispute, denial or doubt', that 'every distinct community or nation of men is owner of itself; and can never of right be bound to submit to be governed by another people'.[35] On these grounds he formulated the classic statement of Irish sovereignty:

> Ireland her own — Ireland her own, and all therein, from the sod to the sky. The soil of Ireland for the people of Ireland, to have and to hold from God alone who gave it — to have and to hold to them and their heirs for ever, without suit or service, faith or fealty, rent or render, to any power under Heaven.[36]

The central claim ('Ireland her own, and all therein from the sod to the sky') is based on a principle of English law which was designed to help the judge or jurist to decide specific property disputes. According to Blackstone:

> Land hath also in its legal signification, an indefinite extent, upwards as well as downwards. *Cujus est solum, ejus est usque ad coelum*, is the maxim of the law, upwards; therefore no man may erect any building, or the like, to overhang another's land; and, downwards, whatever is in the direct line, between the surface of any land and the centre of the earth, belongs to the owner of the surface . . . So that the word "land" includes not only the face of the earth, but everything under it, or over it.[37]

This principle, as can be seen, was designed to clarify who owned what parcels of land in cases involving dispute. Lalor, however, ingeniously inflated it into the general rule that state sovereignty involves 'ownership' of the land by the nation. Because he believed Irish sovereignty so defined to be fundamentally intact, he warned the Irish landlords to give their 'allegiance to this fair isle' or stand accused of treason. 'For a worse crime', he wrote

and more infamous than disloyalty or treason to kings or crowns is disloyalty or treason to country. It is a crime not made by lawyers, but made by God; a crime against nature itself — against all its laws, affections, interests, and instincts.[38]

As the penalty for treason under English law is dispossession, Lalor's tenets are an obvious attack on aristocratic landed property. According to the English law of escheats, when ownership of individual estates fell-in due to treason or the death of an heirless proprietor, the lands thus vacated reverted to the King — the 'sovereign lord or lord paramount, either mediate or immediate of all and every parcel of land within the realm'.[39] To whom would Irish lands revert? Lalor answered this question by altering the legal principle covering reversions in English law from *nullum tempus occurrit regi* to *nullum tempus occurrit populo*.[40] Hence, as the ultimate source of sovereignty, 'the people' are described as the 'lords paramount'[41] and all lands legally vacated revert to them.

It is perhaps for this reason that Lalor has been seen by some as an advocate of land nationalisation.[42] His purpose, in fact, was quite different. The object of his legal arguments on the questions of internal and external sovereignty, and of property rights, was to overthrow the aristocracy by abolishing 'the tenure by which the lands of this country are now holden in fee for the British crown' and, in their stead, to assert 'the true and indefeasible right of property — the right of [the] people to live in this land and possess it — as God and nature intended them to do'. Because 'the landowners have adopted the process of depopulation, and . . . are declaring that they and we can no longer live together in this land', the people in self-defence are enjoined 'to oust and abolish the present noble race of landowners', and to have 'their lands . . . vested in the occupying tenants'. If any landlords agreed 'to swear allegiance to the people of Ireland, and to hold in fee from the Irish nation' they would be granted new titles and suffer 'no eventual or permanent loss'.[43] Lalor, however, did not expect such a situation to arise[44] and only mentioned it as a sop to the Confederation's public policy of a 'union of all classes' (including the aristocracy) in a national movement. However, before drawing any positive conclusions as to how he differed from his co-workers in his appeal to law and in his views of the land question, it will be necessary first to establish the contours and trends of the general 'debate' on the land question and of the part it had to play — or, more precisely, the role prescribed for it — within the prevailing constitutional agitation.

(iii) LAND AND LAW

'I have nothing to do with the landlord-and-tenant question as understood',[45] Lalor wrote to Mitchel in 1847. The warning was apposite in a decade when theories on that thorny problem were more abundant than potatoes.[46] In fact, it seems likely that, even had the disaster of the famine not forced it unavoidably on the attentions of all, the land question would have improved its relative standing in a political arena dominated by the slow demise of the Repeal Association. After the Clontarf debacle of 1843, O'Connell was forced to move in the direction of a more pragmatic, bread-and-butter politics. A major source of propaganda on the land question was duly provided by the Devon Commission,[47] which published a mass of evidence on which all writers subsequently drew in support of their theories.

Relying almost exclusively on this source, the Repeal Association in 1845 drew up three reports on the land question in quick succession.[48] They recommended that the tenant-right of Ulster be extended, 'seeing the prosperity in Ulster' (which they clearly believed was a consequence of the custom), to the other provinces. Besides the suggestion that 'a heavy Absentee Tax' be imposed to stem the presumed flow of money out of the kingdom,[49] they also proposed that *the existing law be amended* in order to facilitate the sale of encumbered estates, and that estates coming on the market be sold not *in toto* as self-contained units but in small lots 'with a right of pre-emption to the occupiers, so as to enable persons possessed of a moderate amount of capital to invest their money in the purchase of land'.[50]

As the post-famine experience was to prove, sale of encumbered estates was not the answer. A free market in land would let the door open for speculators rather than farmers and even granted a right of pre-emption by the tenants there was no guarantee that they could or would avail of an offer which depended on the availability of ready money. At any rate, such measures would not self-evidently improve the condition of 'the labourers and small farmers'. This was to be achieved by the extension of tenant-right, by *legally* compelling 'any occupier of more than 200 acres of grass-land, in any barony, to let a portion of the same annually as con-acre land', and by having 'penal rents . . . declared *illegal*'.[51] Thus, on the very eve of the first season of blight (the reports were presented in April and May 1845) the Repeal Association, despite — or perhaps because of — its adherence to received economic nostrums, viewed the agrarian problem as, essentially, a matter for the law. That the policies which it recommended were deemed necessary at all, was seen as a consequence of the Union, the repeal of which by causing the return and expenditure at home of the money of the country, opening up and developing all her abounding resources, and placing her interests under the guardianship of men living in Ireland, and thoroughly acquainted with Ireland, would ensure the speedy redress of many of the grievances under which the population labour; and in all probability, render unnecessary some of the *legislative interference,* which, under existing circumstances, we find ourselves *compelled to recommend.*[52]

The Association was motivated primarily by its concern for the legal rights of property.[53] Distress provided the fuel for agrarian outrages which threatened property, and in view of the fact that: 'A large proportion of the immediate landlords are so deeply in debt, that their rents cannot be much reduced without ruin to them, and to the far larger class, their creditors', the Association aimed 'to secure to property its just rights', 'to give to the landlords of Ireland a flourishing and contented tenantry, without decreasing their rentals', and 'to encourage the multiplication of small estates in fee, without violating any of the rights of property'.[54] Repealers obviously looked to the State as the arbiter in landlord-tenant relations, though the task with which they charged it, and the policy they recommended were impossible to implement given the fact that they demanded that the 'peasantry' be placated, that the landlords' rentals not be diminished, and that the agrarian system remain, fundamentally, intact. The fact that they looked to the landlords as a possible source of political support (or, at least , as a class which they could alienate only at enormous cost to themselves) meant that their room for manoeuvre on the land question was considerably restricted. In wanting to have their cake and eat it too they received considerable ideological support from Young Ireland.

'On the Tenure Question our course has been an open and decided one', wrote Thomas Davis in 1843.

We seek to secure to the peasant land at a just rent. A just rent would leave him comfort and some leisure.
We seek for him the value of all the labour or money he spends in improvements. And we seek *prospective laws,* which will tend, by a natural and easy change, to reduce the great estates, and create a body of small proprietors in fee throughout every part of Ireland. But we are not ready to jump into a servile war for this purpose.
On the contrary, we shall do our best to make the landlords recognise that the postponement of the tenure settlements or the decline of the political agitation would lead to an anti-rent movement which might end in a disastrous rebellion, but would begin by reducing them to beggary and could not be quelled by the defeat of insurgent armies.[55]

Though Davis was the leading ideologue of the Young Irelanders his statements on this issue were not representative. Duffy, for instance, could declaim against 'the tyranny of property' or exclaim:

Why should landlords be the only class of traders above the law? There is no inherent dignity in selling land more than in selling shoes; and the traders in acres ought to be just as amenable to the law, and just as easily punished for extortion, as his more industrious brother.[56]

Or Michael Doheny might claim, as he 'analysed' 'Crime in Tipperary', that because of the conquest

Usurpation became *sanctified*, rebellion *the constitution,* and robbery *law*. . . Law to [the Irishman] was but a crafty wile, whereby the murder of his race and the plunder of his property were consecrated . . . From those who were the owners of the land all [the People's] woes sprung, and seeing that the laws were made *by* this class, and for their interest, retaliation became a blind vengeance, wreaked alike on the deserving and undeserving of that class.[57]

Or John Dillon, a co-founder of the *Nation* and to date the object of an inscrutable silence, might analyse and condemn Irish society in general, and 'Aristocratic institutions' in particular, by applying the Benthamite calculus of good and evil:

The end of laws is human happiness. Every law which produces, on the whole, more happiness than misery is wise and just, and it is our duty to obey it. Every law which produces, on the whole, more misery than happiness, [which Dillon believed to be the case in Ireland] is wicked and unjust, and it is our duty to resist it, or at least to insist that it be abolished.[58]

Clearly, Young Ireland was not homogeneous. Yet, regardless of individual differences of emphasis or approach, all would have agreed with Duffy that as 'friends of the people' they did not 'demand justice from individuals, but from the State' on the grounds that 'the public good is the business of the State'.[59] Moreover, though for Young Irelanders the landlord-tenant question was primarily a legal matter, it was also, essentially, a social issue. It is therefore important to note that, as Davis could put it:

Nationality was our first great object. *All* social and political movements we valued only as they promoted it; and from it alone we sought, and do expect to gain, social and political prosperity for Ireland.[60]

Few commentators or agitators shared Young Ireland's faith in or appeal to the panacea of nationality. Almost all, on the other hand, looked to the State as the final arbiter on the land question. William Sharman Crawford, for instance, worked untiringly in the House of Commons to have the tenant's right to compensation for improvements recognised by law.[61] To that end he introduced a succession of (defeated) bills until, in 1843, he received an undertaking from Peel 'that the Government would be disposed to give a fair consideration to the subject', adding the significant rider that 'they would discountenance any expectation that they meant to recognize in any shape or form what was called fixity of tenure, or any alienation of the rights of the landlords'.[62]

Fixity of tenure — otherwise known at the time as the 'tenant right of occupancy' — was the essence of William Conner's programme.[63] Rack-rents, he believed, were the cause of the evils inherent in the landlord-tenant relationship, and he advocated 'a valuation and perpetuity as its only effectual remedy'. In addressing the tenants in 1832 he proposed:

> that the legislature should interpose on your behalf by passing a Bill for the applotment or valuation of land, by which all lands already let, or hereafter to be let, shall be brought down to their fair value, so that instead of, as heretofore, the whole of your crop, and even the pig, the horse, and the cow, from your door, going to pay a desolating rack-rent, a fair and full proportion of all shall be left for the consumption and support of the farmer, labourer, and all engaged in the cultivation of the soil. And that this fair value of land being once fixed by a sworn jury of men, all acreable assessments, and all charges of whatever kind or amount on the land, and paid by you in the first instance, shall afterwards be considered as so much of the rent discharged. Thus protecting you in the outset from the cruel oppression of an all devouring rack-rent, and then from all charges levied on the land.[64]

In appealing to the State to interfere in the market-place Conner is aware, though neither Repealers nor Young Irelanders seem to be, that he might be attacked for upsetting the *laissez-faire* apple cart:

> Here, [he argues in defence of his proposals] is a loaf of bread on my table, I would get it for three pence, but by an act of Parliament I must pay six pence, is not this a good smart interference of the legislature, with the rights of private property.[65]

Despite the variety of participants, the 'debate' on the land question (insofar as there was one) not only failed to break through the matrix of constitutional politics, but also, and essentially, was *legalist* in its approach and in its details. In looking to the State as the final arbiter, all land-agitators and pamphleteers were, in fact, in tune with the reformist spirit of the age which sought redress by petitioning Westminster.

(iv) CONCLUSIONS

Law and the recourse to none but legal means had been the policy of O'Connell and it had struck deep roots. Though reform of individual statutes was considered not only possible but essential, all endeavours for redress were based on a profound respect for the law and its institutions. Not that the law was seen as impervious but that reform of anomalies needed to be approached gingerly and with circumspection. Blackstone had once characterised the legal edifice as 'an old Gothic castle, erected in the days of chivalry, but fitted up for a modern inhabitant'.[66] In remodelling it and increasing its comfort, a reverential care was necessary lest, unwittingly, the reformers should 'loosen an apparently useless stone or weaken some inconvenient timber and cause the whole edifice, the pleasant apartments as well as the noble shell, vital damage'.[67]

In his use of the law, Lalor was less circumspect than most. His contemporaries petitioned the government for the reform of certain laws or the abrogation of others (Repealers, Young Ireland, the Confederation); they sought legal recognition of existing customs (Crawford); or State involvement as a regulator in the market-place (Conner); and, as a result of such policies and recommendations, they anticipated a better rural regime in Ireland in the future. The law, or to be precise, the individual statute, came first and the fruits of redress followed. Lalor, on the other hand, sought a complete over-haul of the law, *and* its absolute transplantation to Irish conditions. In sum, he differed from his contemporaries in that, whilst they were exclusively concerned with the 'legal superstructure', he concentrated on its 'philosophic foundations'.[68]

He argued publicly and privately, in his correspondence with the Confederationists and in the pages of the *Felon*, that 'the principle I assert would make Ireland in fact as she is of *right*, the mistress and queen of all [Irish] lands';[69] a point he had previously made, though in reverse order, to Mitchel: 'To show [the aristocracy] we are owners *de jure*, we have only to prove that we are owners *de facto*'.[70] For Lalor, independence was a fact of law and of history. In face of conquest, however, it needed constant reassertion. It was for this reason that he occasionally advocated force. But, and the *caveat* is important, he urged the use of force in circumstances of 'utter and desperate necessity *to fortify* [*Ireland's*] *claim, but not to found it*'.[71] Its foundation was secured in legal and moral terms as an inalienable *right*.

The question of sovereign independence was, because of colonisation, inextricably bound up with the land question. It was the latter which really consumed Lalor's energies. Concerned mainly with the plight of the small holders he endeavoured to secure their claims to the land by founding them in law; a policy which entailed, as a necessary corollary, an attack on aristocratic titles to Irish land. His arguments were both ingenious and radical and mark him apart from his contemporaries not only for his broad grasp of legal principles, but also for his open and consistent attacks on the aristocracy.

The Confederation, like Young Ireland before it, was capable of the occasional outburst against the lords and gentry. However, their primary political credo was that nothing could possibly be done on the land question until a 'union of all classes' (including the aristocracy) into one cohesive nation had been achieved. Because the Confederation in '47 had rejected his tenets, and his policy of a rent-strike, Lalor whipped them publicly for their folly in the following year. 'They chose', he wrote in the *Felon*,

> to consider [the landowners] as Irishmen, and imagined they could induce them to hoist the green flag. They wished to preserve an Aristocracy. They desired not a *democratic* but a merely *national* revolution.[72]

A democratic revolution would be 'a Social war of extermination', fought between the aristocrats and the people, from which the former 'would come out the losers, whoever might be the winners'. The central issue in that struggle would be landownership and Lalor had no doubt that 'the people [would emerge as] lords of the land, a mighty social revolution [would be] accomplished, and the foundations of a national revolution [would be] surely laid'.[73]

However, as Lalor is by no means clear in his use of terms, it will be necessary, before going any further, to consider the implications of his terminology. Popular sovereignty is clear enough provided the semi-mystical nature of sovereignty is taken for granted. But what exactly did Lalor mean by 'the people'? Though it is feasible to imagine every individual having, at least, a say in selecting representatives who would govern Ireland, are we to understand also that they would each have a share in the land? Or, as seems more likely, would the mystical entity 'the people' merely confer new national titles on those who already possessed the land? As we shall see, 'the people' were not homogeneous and the clash between them and the aristocracy was but one of a variety of conflicts inherent in the make-up of Irish society.

3

Lalor's Use of 'Class'

(i) THE EMERGENCE OF 'CLASS'

Edmund Burke, in keeping with his role as arch-propagandist of, and for, the old order, would have thought the politics of 'class' an absurd impertinence,[1] a fiction, created by the French and Industrial Revolutions, which had no *legal* base and which, therefore, was null and void. For the over-riding fact of the *ancien régime* — with its elaborate vocabulary of 'ranks', 'orders', 'degrees', 'estates', and (economic) 'interests', its pyramidal structure of landed aristocratic/noble 'status' and propertyless/mass 'dependence' (and, hence, deference) — was its entrenched legal foundation.[2] This was, however, a view of society and of politics which became increasingly anachronistic in the years after Burke put pen to paper. Even if the French Revolution had not occurred to goad his counter-revolutionary pen, industrialisation and urbanisation in England would have swamped his defence of paternalistic, aristocratic rule. The language and politics of 'class' would still have emerged whilst those of 'rank' and 'privilege' would have retreated (as they did) into the squirearchical, antiquarian wing of Conservative Party politics.

'Class' was not a new term but its specific use in socio-political contexts in the period from 1770 to 1840 (roughly coterminous, that is, with the Industrial Revolution) marks it apart as the most convenient linguistic barometer of the re-organisation, upheaval and change which characterised that period. '*Class* is a more indefinite word than *rank*', according to Raymond Williams, who feels that 'this was probably one of the reasons for its introduction'.[3] There is, however, rather more to the phenomenon than this would suggest. In the old order, 'rank' and 'status' had been part of the formal, self-conscious vocabulary of Aristocratic domination whereby the dependant People had been assigned passive roles by those who monopolised power. The Industrial Revolution, however, had smashed the deferential matrix and substituted what Carlyle had called 'the cash nexus'.[4] The impersonal market became the broker of the new society. Old tags were cashed-in for new, and the new were as much definitions *vis-à-vis* the market as they were demarcations *vis-à-vis* other social groups. In the new order, 'class' (for all its failings, ambiguities, and inconsistencies) became primarily and essentially a vocabulary of *self-consciousness* developed by 'the People', the hitherto deferential stratum of the traditional social pyramid.

The *nouveau riche*, the capitalist middle class, were the first to extricate themselves, as a group, from the dependant role assigned them in the old, hierarchical pyramid. For the working class, which regarded itself as comprising the bulk of 'the People', Lord Brougham's appropriation of that tag for the exclusive use of the middle classes was an incomprehensible absurdity: 'By the people, I mean the middle classes, the wealth and intelligence of the country, and the glory of the British name'.[5] It was only *after* the 1832 Reform Bill that working class disaffection became *class* conscious. As the aristocracy could no longer be viewed as the sole barrier to truly radical reform measures, spokesmen for the working class redefined the terms of the struggle. As a result, they included a section of the middle classes (the capitalists) as a new element in the barrier to reform. 'The enemy', as Patricia Hollis could put it, 'was capitalist economics rather than Aristocratic privilege, property rather than taxes, a profiteering middle class rather than a parasitic upper class'.[6] It was no accident that one of the best English working class newspapers of the nineteenth century was named *The Bee-Hive.*[7] It symbolised, at one level, the common belief that the masses toiled for the benefit of the few. It symbolised also, and most succinctly, the impersonal drudgery of work and the poor rewards it gave to labour. Out of the common stock of honey they received least who produced most. The hive as a nexus cheated the worker of the fruits of his toil. All these symbolic meanings (and there were others) were in keeping with a view of society which ranged the 'industrious classes' against the indolent and opulent few.[8] It was from this re-appraisal that the familiar tripartite model of society, composed of Aristrocracy (Upper Class), Capitalists (Middle Class), and Labour (Working Class), emerged.

It is clear from the nature of the terminology that the descriptive, pyramidal model — originally composed of the Aristocracy and an amorphous group called 'the People' — survived the transition from the *ancient régime* to the modern world, though the strata which it contained were both more diverse and less deferential. The new vocabulary reflected changed social conditions. Yet, despite its egalitarian elements, it was not (as some historians contend) a horizontal, but a vertical model.[9] The new terminology, in fact, retained and perpetuated that sense of hierarchy which had been a hallmark of its predecessor. What had changed was not the existence but the *awareness* of a pecking order. Industrialisation and urbanisation were instrumental in creating that awareness.

Given that Ireland was not experiencing similar social upheavals, how then are we to account for the emergence of class terminology in that country in the same period? Quite simply, the decline of Gaelic together with the Act of Union created the conditions in which the vocabulary of class, once established in England, could migrate. Select committees and parliamentary reports were an obvious channel for the dissemination of the new terminology.[10] In addition, as Westminster provided the focus for parallel reform movements in both islands, the possibilities for overlap — and 'plagiarism' — were greatly enhanced. Nor was the traffic all one way. The apparent absurdity of 'modern' class terminology applied to a 'traditional' Irish society and economy was matched by the utopian agricultural schemes sponsored by the Chartist Land Plan.[11] In fact neither trend was as anachronistic as it might seem. Chartism was a response to economic dislocation. The Land Plan was therefore an attempt to provide a *secure* livelihood for those thrown on the mercy of the new market. Similarly, 'class' terminology was not redundant once it crossed the Irish Sea. It was simply adapted to meet different circumstances. In the process, it lost that neat, monolithic uniformity which in large measure had been its strength in England. At any rate, by the mid-forties 'class' was firmly established in common parlance in Ireland. It was evident not only in select committees and parliamentary reports but in pamphlets,[12] newspapers,[13] and magazines.[14] It was most often used as a general, descriptive term without 'conflict', or ideological underpinnings. For some individuals, however, it had specific and perceptible contours.

(ii) NATIONALITY AND CLASS

In 1869, Marx — who saw the Irish question as a lever to ensure 'working-class ascendancy' in England — was incensed by 'the stupidity and wretchedness of the *Irish* leaders in Dublin'. The First International was about to have a general debate on the Irish problem but nationalist leaders, it seems, were not impressed. In fact, the debate was not even mentioned in the columns of the native press. Marx, predictably, saw red. In a Promethean fury he wrote to Engles castigating Irish leaders in general, but Richard Pigott (editor of *The Irishman*) in particular. He affected incredulity that Pigott, an 'ass' and 'a stupid beast', could dare to myopically turn his back on the International 'which has press organs all over Europe and the United States!'[15] Engels was less sanguinary. Soothingly he reminded Marx that for 'these gentry the whole labour movement is a heresy'. He simultaneously deflated the 'honest madness' of Irish nationalists and Marx's unreasonable rage with a deftly administered and pungent jab: 'Ireland', he wrote, with luminous sarcasm, 'still remains the *sacra insula*, whose aspirations must on no account be mixed up with the profane class struggles of the rest of the sinful world'.[16]

Obsessed with the grand strategy of global class revolution Marx was blinkered and, hence, at a considerable disadvantage when dealing with the reality of the Irish situation.[17] Engels, being less doctrinaire, was often not only more informed but more realistic. He was less likely to treat Irish nationalists, or the political tactics they employed, as evidence of deliberate obscurantism. Indeed, the tone of his letters suggests that he respected, though he did not share, the outlook and motives of Irish politicians. The latter, for their part, were certainly anxious to put as much distance as was possible between themselves and the International. This, however, does not mean that the politics of class were redundant in Ireland. Quite the contrary, in fact; class analyses of Irish society abounded.

Lalor's father, for instance, claimed to discern 'three classes of landlords' and 'three classes' of tenants in Ireland: the former comprising proprietors (largely aristocrats), middlemen (largely Catholics) and the courts (i.e., institutional or State holdings); and the latter consisting simply of large farmers, small farmers, and labourers. Of the three types of landlord, Lalor (himself a middleman) declared:

> Much has been said against middlemen in their capacity of landlords, but I am certain I see many of them having more comfortable tenants than any under any proprietor. . . . There is not that distance between the middleman and his tenants as between the proprietor and the tenant:[18]

Therefore, in order to escape the clutches of fleecing agents — also in his view a class in themselves[19] — and to avoid the temptation to become (inexplicable as this seems) 'more extravagant and wasteful of their time and their money' as tenants to aristocratic landlords,[20] Lalor encouraged farmers to take land under middlemen — even though the latter charged 'a higher rent'![21] These arguments would seem to imply not only that middlemen are more aware of the needs of their tenants, but also that the latter are incapable of properly managing their holdings and their lives unless guided by benevolent overseers. In addition, Lalor claims that tenants holding directly from aristocratic landlords are obliged to toe a public, political line which they do not privately espouse.[22] The implication is that this would *not* be the case were they to take land under middlemen. Yet (though Lalor does not seem to be aware of the inconsistency), he is clearly advising tenants to substitute one form of patron-client relationship for another, and to do so by paying a higher rent for the reduced social distance involved. In any event, Lalor clearly believes that either the aristocracy or the middlemen must take the peasants in hand, for they are incapable of sober (and solvent) management of their affairs on their own initiative.

However, the tenantry were not viewed as a homogeneous bloc. They also comprised 'three classes' — large farmers, small farmers, and labourers — all three of which were 'with few exceptions, in debt to their respective landlords, and to as many others as will give them credit'.[23] Nor were the labourers the worst off. In Lalor's view there was a lower stratum of 'poorer classes' from which the labourers themselves held land. The entire agricultural system was weighed down by rents, taxes, crown rents, poor rate, county cess, road and other imposts, and a whole litany of minor leeches. In addition, those on the land were either at the mercy of respectable banks or, at the bottom of the rural ladder, of local usurers. The crowning ignominy of the whole system, Lalor claimed as a loyal repealer, was the lack of 'an independent legislature [to] foster our manufactures, our trade, our commerce, and our fisheries, each and all of which [would] provide remunerative employment'.[24]

Despite the world of differences which separated him from 'Honest Pat' Lalor, Davis too expounded a class theory — of sorts. In his 'Address delivered before the historical society' in Trinity College, he referred to his audience as 'the upper classes', and warned them that the 'middle classes' were jostling for a share in power:

> When the men of the middle class once come into the field, if I do not greatly overrate the stuff of which they are made, they will compel the men of the upper classes at home — nay, with humility be it said, the men of every country — to fight a hard battle for their literary laurels and political renown.[25]

Not only was continued aristocratic domination of education and (hence?) of politics under attack from the middle classes, but the National Schools were, in addition, raising the educational horizons and, thereby, the political expectations of the 'lower classes':

I tell you, gentlemen of Trinity College, the peasant boys will soon put to the proof your title to lead them, and the only title likely to be acknowledged in the people-court is that which our countryman, himself once a peasant boy, ascribes to Pericles —

> "He waved the sceptre o'er his kind
> By Nature's first great title — mind".[26]

Davis did not foresee an age in which 'the peasant boys' would also seek a share in political power. His sole, naïve, idealistic expectation was that, thanks to the meliorating influence of the National Schools, intellectual considerations alone ('mind') would dictate the peasantry's choice of political representatives. Though he also professed *en passant* a belief in 'democracy [as] the undoubted basis of free government', he was unsure 'whether a social equality should or indeed could be added to the political'. Nevertheless, he said, he shared 'the conviction that all classes in the country should be left to their own natural development; only taking care that no matter how connected with, or dependent on, each other, they [should], if possible, be independent of the stranger'.[27]

The tri-partite model of upper, middle, and lower classes which Davis had used in the 'Address', was later dropped in favour of a more traditional, pyramidal structure comprising 'Lords, Gentry, [and] Commonality'.[28] In this model Davis reverted to the old 'Aristrocracy versus the People' typology which, as we have seen, had been the common parlance of English radical politics in the first two decades of the century. This neat, and in many respects, naïve 'We/They' dichotomy had been largely superseded in the 1830s by the embryo of modern socialist analysis: viz., a tri-partite division into Aristocracy, Capitalists and Labour. Thus, Davis deliberately went against the chronological grain. Why? We know that he had in fact flirted with English radical politics prior to his involvement in either *The Nation* or Repeal. However, though he never entirely eschewed class-analysis, his advocacy of nationalism represented a deliberate, and diametrically opposed, policy. It was not so much that class concepts proved inapplicable for his purposes, as that national identity and related problems began to monopolise his energies. As Kee has remarked,

Irishness was something which the Catholic O'Connell did not need to think about intellectually for it was such a recognizable part of him and his long family tradition. But for Davis, the son of an English army surgeon and an Irish mother . . . Irishness was something which he found he consciously needed to work out and acquire for his own self-respect.[29]

The theory that Davis propounded as a result was based on compromise and community rather than conflict and class. He appealed for 'a Nationality of the spirit as well as the letter . . . which may embrace Protestant, Catholic, and Dissenter — Milesian and Cromwellian — the Irishman of a hundred generations and the stranger who is within our gates'.[30] Anxious to paper over the cracks which would hinder the realisation of this non-sectarian ideal, Davis eschewed class explanations in favour of a unified nationalist structure. Like Gavan Duffy, he sought an alliance between the aristocracy and the middle class.[31] However, the attempted reconciliation of classes in the interests of the Irish Nation was by no means easy, especially as Davis (no less than his contemporaries) was aware of the 'brilliant vices of the Aristocracy'[32] and of the rising tide of criticism which identified them as the main barrier to progress.

In his 'nationalist' analysis, therefore, though he employed a tri-partite division into nobles, gentry, and people, what was important was not the arrangement into 'classes', but the super-imposition of a Patriots versus Traitors dividing line which cut across the 'class' boundaries and, to all intents and purposes, rendered them null and void. Thus the nobles were 'the highest class', and were sub-divided into those who have 'worked, struggled, sacrificed for Ireland' (presumably the minority?) and 'those, or their descendants, who, at the time of the Union, sold their country and the high places they filled in her councils and in her glory, for the promise of a foreign title'.[33] Similarly, according to Davis, the gentry also are

divisible into two classes — the one consists of the old Norman race commingled with the Catholic gentlemen who either have been able to maintain their patrimonies, or who have risen into affluence by their own industry; the other, the descendants of Cromwell's or William's successful soldiery.[34]

For Davis these last were 'the most anti-Irish of all', for they acted as though it was 'their interest as well as their duty to degrade, and wrong, and beggar the Irish people'.[35] Thus, in keeping with the old pyramidal model of society which he had adopted, Davis saw 'the people' — that bedrock of undifferentiated, axiomatic patriots — as the broad base on which the entire structure rested:

The people of this country are its wealth [he declared]. They till its soil, raise its produce, ply its trade. They serve, sustain, support, save it. They supply its armies — they are its farmers, its merchants, its tradesmen, its artists, all that enrich and adorn it.[36]

Perhaps the single most important aspect of Davis' view of class structure is its moral base. In his 'Address', the rise of the middle-classes and the educational improvement of the lower-classes (both of which he sees as aspects of the challenge to aristocratic domination) are also trends which he finds unsettling:

The people are pressing on in a career certain of sweeping away every law and custom which impedes their physical comfort, though in doing so they may overthrow some of the barriers which protect their morals, and therefore guard their happiness.[37]

It is because he sees man as 'a moral and imaginative being, beyond "the reasoning, self-sufficing thing" ', that Davis deliberately ignores the conflict which underlies class theory and takes his stand instead on 'the moral principles by which society is tied together'.[38] It is this moral conviction, in addition, which gives his high-principled nationalism its distinctively Keatsian flavour. What is dominant is the romantic reverence for virtue, purity, nobility (of character), and epic enterprises; 'the holiness of the heart's affections', as Keats could put it.

For Duffy, who was perhaps neither as romantic as Davis, nor as adept in using class terminology, Irish society revealed itself as a series of more-or-less powerful political constituencies:

For, know this fact [he declared] — never lose sight of it, or you may as well attempt to speculate on the condition of the men on the moon as on that of the men of Connemara — the agricultural classes *cannot agitate this question for themselves*. If the towns will not agitate for them, they have nothing to do but to suffer and be dumb.[39]

For Duffy there were but two political agencies in Ireland. The landlords and gentry were the rural (and ruling) constituency. Their oppressed tenants, having no political voice, would have to gain their leadership from the only other constituency available: the towns. 'It was my rooted conviction which time amply justified' he wrote in 1883,

that some at least of the gentry, and the young men of the middle class as a body, were indispensable: without them we could neither gain our end in peace or war. It was they who made the revolutions the world was proudest to recall.[40]

By comparison with either Davis or Duffy, Meagher, the son of a wealthy Waterford merchant and a product of Clongowes and Stonyhurst, was a bundle of ambiguities and contradictions. 'I am one of the people', he declared in 1847,

> but I am no democrat. I am for an equality of civil rights — but I am no republican. I am for vesting the responsibilities and the duties of government in three estates. I think that in a free state, an aristocracy is a wise — an enobling institution . . . I can conceive no state complete without it.[41]

Inclined to give impassioned speeches in which he envisaged 'armed columns of the peasantry' being *led* to glory (and, though he never mentioned it, almost certain death) behind the banners of that 'wild and glittering passion', patriotism, Meagher yet saw no contradiction in describing the 'peasant population' and the 'mechanic population' as the

> two great classes — that form the very nerve and marrow of [the] nation — without which there is, in fact, no nation to be saved — without which a professional class is so much parchment and powdered horsehair — and a nobility a mere glittering spectre.[42]

Though he preferred the language of 'ranks' and 'orders', Meagher began to use class terminology, awkwardly and for the first time, in the late 1840s. At about the same time, Fr John Kenyon (a friend of Fintan Lalor) also partially intermixed the language of peers, people, sects and orders with that of class. In February 1848, for instance, he declared to Mitchel that he 'despair[ed] of a unity of classes in Ireland', though he shows how unfamiliar the term is by talking of 'the military class', and by using 'the landlord class' as a synonym for the 'order . . . of landed proprietors'. His class convictions, however, are definitely those of Young Ireland. The 'middle classes, whether tradesmen or shopkeepers', he alleges (referring indirectly to Lalor's tenant politics, which he distrusts) constitute, 'such as they are, the worth and hope of Ireland, as well and truly, in my judgement, as the corresponding class of tenant farmers'.[43] Middle class élitism and middle class leadership were central to Young Ireland's policies, whether of moral or of physical force. However, though loosely used, 'middle class' usually implied (consciously or not) that only the urban constituency could act on behalf of the unpoliticised, rural masses. Lalor was the only agitator in '48 who looked to the tenant farmers as 'the worth and hope of Ireland'.

(iii) LALOR'S USE OF 'CLASS'

Whilst privately confiding to Mitchel that he 'never recognised the landowners as an element, or as part and portion of the Irish nation',[44] Fintan

Lalor was publicly arguing in *The Nation* (in compliance with Duffy's editorial line) that a reconciliation of classes in the interests of Ireland could only be accomplished if based on a new social contract. To enable such a contract to be formed, however, the ground had first to be cleared: 'There are many important questions at issue between you [aristocrats] and the landholders, between you and the labourers, between you and the people, between you and other classes of the people, between those classes among themselves'.[45] Far from being a simple case of the 'Aristocracy versus the People', therefore, what emerges now is a plethora of conflicting interests, each ranged against the other. 'The People' are not homogeneous; or rather, to be more precise, Lalor is forced to admit that popular grievances against the aristocracy are not the only internal conflicts in Irish society. A series of no less important petty-contracts must be entered into between the landholders, the labourers, and every other class of 'The People'.

The-People-with-a-capital-'P' can therefore be reduced to its component classes. The divisions which Lalor employs, however, are purely idiosyncratic. They lack the 'scientific', dialectical inter-relationships which Marx, for example, enumerates in his class theory. In addition, Lalor's class stratification is implicit; that is, it is not presented as a coherent abstract theory, but is employed as an analytical tool to explicate *specific* social ills in a *specific* country. It is, thus, not part of a vast, universally-applicable ideological framework.[46] However, it is a more dense stratification than Davis' neat tri-partite structure and, as used by Lalor, can be approached and examined in terms of any of the following parameters:

(a) — In terms of power (itself a concept which changes its colours many times in Lalor's writings);
(b) — In terms of political articulateness;
(c) — In terms of an Urban/Rural divide; and,
(d) — In terms of relationship to the land.

For Lalor the power-matrix is essentially one of socio-political privilege, or lack of same. Under the pre-famine regime it rested largely, and virtually exclusively, in the hands of the aristorcracy. They possessed 'power of position', an exclusive social status which was mirrored in the political arena. As landlords they owned the soil, were socially superior to their tenants, monopolised economic power, and occupied the more lucrative rungs on the social ladder. 'The People', on the other hand, had the power of superior numbers ('they number more in millions than you do in thousands'). They possessed also, due to the failure of the aristocracy to 'provide for its people', a monopoly of moral power: viz., the fact that the aristocracy had reneged on its duties to the people meant that 'In the case that has arisen the main power is in [the people's] hands . . . The right is in them because the power is in them. The right lodges where the power lodges'.[47] This was not to assert that might was right, that numerical strength validated all claims for change. On the contrary, power (like sovereignty) has, for Lalor, a semi-mystical base in the fundamental inalienable rights of individuals. The social collapse consequent on famine reached its theoretical nadir at this level. Any attempt at reconstruction had, therefore, to take into explicit account the existence of such rights and to use them as the base and building blocks of any future society.

From the perspective of political articulateness, the People could be subdivided into those who, like Lalor, were eminently capable of demanding their rights in the face of any political threat. Thus, in his first letter to *The Nation*, (addressed ostensibly to the landlords, but with occasional lengthy asides to 'the public') he stressed that he addressed his 'betters' as an equal, and that he did not come begging, cap in hand, for attentive silence: 'that I am excited by and authorised by the feelings and emergencies of the occasion. This is my claim to a hearing. Not that I ask it in my own cause or in that of the class I belong to.'[48]

At the other end of the spectrum were those 'masses of men unable to ask [a hearing] for themselves',[49] the inarticulate multitude beyond the pale of class politics. Without a voice — other than those, perhaps, of emigration, starvation, and (most important of all) all agrarian outrage — they had no defenders. Lalor clearly saw himself as the protector of this amorphous mass of humanity; whether from self-interest or a high-minded philanthropy is difficult to assess. One suspects the former; especially as this inarticulate mass emerges into something resembling the light of day when viewed from the Urban versus Rural standpoint.

The urban political classes were identified by Lalor as those which supported O'Connell: 'Repeal', he wrote, 'is the Question of the town population'. Opposite them were the agricultural political classes, whose social and political demands were forever being forced to play second fiddle to those of the urban élites: 'the land tenure question', he concluded, 'is that of the country peasantry'.[50] This urban/rural dichotomy might seem unrealistic given the country and the times with which Lalor was dealing; however, there *was* ample reason to fear that the tenure question might be taken up and betrayed by O'Connell's Repeal Association, in much the same way, perhaps, as the Tithe War — an agricultural, political issue — had been stifled by the Liberator in the 1830s. To cite but one example, Duffy's élitist, urban conviction that the agricultural classes could not agitate for themselves and were thus a constituency without a voice, validates Lalor's anxieties. For, like most Young Irelanders and Repealers, Duffy was apt to treat grass-roots rural unrest as so much cannon fodder in the arguments for repeal, or as a stick with which to beat the aristocracy: *of course* (Duffy would have agreed) the condition of the peasantry was terrible; *of course* it required amelioration, if not outright change. But — and this was the rock on which Young Ireland's policies perished — as social ills were, in their eyes, a consequence of the political situation, nothing could be done until repeal had been gained. Then, everything would be possible; meanwhile, the landlords were the only rural, political constituency. Being middle class themselves, Young Irelanders and Repealers could, and did, argue for middle class participation in power without ever wishing to extend their arguments down the social ladder. For Fintan Lalor this position was untenable, not only because the nobility would never condescend to share power with its middle-class social inferiors, but because the urban-dominated political agitations of Young Ireland and the Repeal Association failed to take into account the fact that the 'agricultural class . . . must precede and provide for every other. It is the first in order of nature, necessity, and time'.[51]

The 'agricultural class', however, was no more homogeneous than 'The People'. Besides the aristocracy, it also contained a 'class of gentlemen farmers'[52] (which included Lalor's father, Patrick); the tenant farmers of ten acres or less, 'the most numerous and important [class] in Ireland'; the cottiers, or 'labourers with allotments'; and, at the bottom of the ladder, the 'independent labourers', the nadir of downward social mobility. Relationship to the land was, thus, the final limiting parameter which defined class. However, whereas the preceding parameters — of power, political articulateness, and of an urban/rural divide — were imprecise, that of land was arithmetically exact. In very general terms Lalor often posed the problem thus:

> It is a mere question between a people and a class — between a people of eight million and a class of eight thousand. They or we must quit the island. It is a people to be saved or lost — it is the island to be kept or surrendered.[53]

In sub-dividing 'the people' into numerically coherent classes, however, Lalor dealt only with the extremes: the aristocracy at the apex, and the labourers and 'small occupiers' at the baseline. The intervening strata (the middle classes?) were not the subject of arithmetical computations. Lalor's classifications and figures are as follows:

Aristocracy .... 8,000 persons[54]
Adult male (wage) labourers ....319,000 persons
Landholders from one acre to ten ....510,000 persons
Holders beyond ten acres each ....370,000 persons

The last two figures are based on the contention that: 'The cultivated soil of Ireland is distributed, or was distributed last year, into about 880,000 land-holdings, each occupied by a family'.[55] This was written in May 1847, and so could not have been based on the agricultural statistics for that year (collected in August) which enumerated some 803,025 holdings.[56] The most obvious source would appear to have been the Devon Commission which included data provided by the Poor Law Commissioners stating that there were 935,448 persons holding land in Ireland in 1844.[57] Of these, 505,173 held 'farms' of ten acres or under. This is reasonably close to Lalor's figure of 510,000 occupiers in 'farms varying in size from one to ten acres'.[58] Strictly speaking one to ten acre holdings amounted to 369,859 according to the Commission's figures but Lalor's descriptive heading changes in the course of his arguments from 'farms varying in size from one to ten acres' to 'the landholders of ten acres or under'[59] (i.e. including 'farms' of less than one acre). We may take it, however, that his figures are reasonably close to the official returns on this point — assuming that the Devon Commission was his source.

However, to arrive at a Commission figure for the total number of holdings which would bear comparison with Lalor's 880,000 a peculiar and arbitrary piece of arithmetic is necessary. The total number of persons holding 100 acres or less, according to the Commission, amounted to 879,968. This is a mere 32 short of Lalor's figure of 880,000. However, to arrive at such a figure would have involved a conscious decision on Lalor's part to omit the additional 25,041 landholders whose estates ranged in size from (over) 100 acres to 5,000 acres. (This does not include the 6 land-holders beyond the 5,000 acre bracket, an obvious under-numeration in the Poor Law Commissioners' figures). The presentation of returns as printed by the Devon Commission does not self-evidently suggest a 'natural' breakpoint at the 100 acre mark, and there is nothing in Lalor's writings which would validate or explicate such a choice.

In addition, Lalor's contention that: 'There are in Ireland, or were last year, 231,000 agricultural families, comprising 319,000 adult male labourers, depending altogether on wages for subsistence'[60] has no foundation in the official figures. According to the 1841 census returns 921,576 families were reported as 'depending on their own manual labour'.[61] Though many of these, undoubtedly, were cottiers and small holders, the latter surely did not account for 75% of the total — for, that's how far we would have to reduce the official figure to arrive at Lalor's estimate. The census of 1841 was, therefore, no this source. Nor can we assume that he referred to the (generally unreliable) census of 1831, according to which 'Labourers employed in agriculture' totalled 567,441.[62] Whereas the most reasonable assumption would be that their number *increased* in the ensuing decade, Lalor's figures would have us believe the reverse was the case. The available evidence, therefore, indicates that he was significantly adrift in the figures he cites; in particular, that labourers were numerically more prominent than he suggests.

Clearly, Lalor's use of statistical material is suspect. His claim that he quotes 'from recollection' having 'no returns at hand to refer to', is no defence, for the Devon Commission volumes were, almost certainly, to hand at Tinakill.[63] In addition, internal inconsistencies and ambiguities undermine any confidence in his statistical abilities. For instance, he claims that, as a result of the famine and of landlord policy, the small holders will be swept off the land to swell the ranks of the 'independent laburers'. This may well be true, but his manner of conveying the statistical dimension of the upheaval leaves much to be desired:

> Five hundred thousand families added to the two hundred and thirty thousand who form the present mass of labour — *six hundred and seventy thousand* adult males converted into 'independent labourers' — six hundred and seventy thousand hands *added to* those three hundred and nineteen thousand already so successfully engaged in independent labour.[64]

At first sight Lalor appears to have gotten his arithmetic wrong: 500,000 + 230,000 = 670,000! However, this is not so. He has simply confused himself and his readers by referring to 'families' and 'adult male labourers' in contexts in which they should be rigorously isolated. Thus, the 500,000 *families* on farms of ten acres or less 'comprise' 670,000 adult *male* labourers; and the 230,000 *families* 'comprising 319,000 adult *male* labourers' constitute the current reservoir of 'landless labourers'. So, when the landholders of ten acres or less are driven off the land, they will increase that pool or landless proletarians by at least 670,000 hands. This relatively simple scenario is unnecessarily complicated by Lalor's cavalier mistreatment (and confusing) of the relevant categories. In addition, he has a disconcerting habit of rounding off his numbers: thus, the 231,000 labouring families are inexplicably reduced to 230,000, whereas the 500,000 small holders had originally been reported as 510,000 families.[65]

Granted, neither his concertina samples, nor his cavalier disregard for his basic statistical units ('families' versus 'labourers') seriously undermines his class argument — but they do erode it. That he rushes into print without either checking his data or providing source references, also damages the 'objective' nature of his claims. Indeed, Lalor's statistical excesses may tend to suggest that his arguments (and vocabulary) have more to do with numerical 'classification' than with social 'classes' rightly understood. To some extent this is true, but it is not an invalidating argument. 'Class', in its primary sense, meant (and means) an agglomeration of individuals within certain defined limits. Objectively, such 'classes' are capable, at least in theory, of numerical definition.

(iv) CONCLUSIONS

Lalor's appeal to 'class' was idiosyncratic. Despite the fact that 'class' formed part of the current vocabulary of rhetoric and dispute up to and beyond the '40s, no writer of the period — and certainly none within Lalor's limited circle — used the terminology with such consistency. Whilst Davis and his heterogeneous coterie were apt to undermine the use of 'class' by appeals to a literary and romanticised 'nationality', Lalor did not follow suit. If Young Irelanders in general were primarily concerned with wooing aristocratic support, Lalor was not. He looked down, not up, the social ladder in search of a constituency, and he attacked the aristocracy *as a class*, not as a segmented order divided into patriots and traitors.

However, the question remains: to what extent did Lalor see 'the people' as political agents in their own right? If Duffy believed that the unprivileged rural masses could only find leaders among the urban élite, to whom did Lalor look for leadership of the same constituency? 'Men are moved only in masses', he wrote in 1847, 'and it is easier to convert a million of men than a single man'.[66] To 'command success' any movement looking for popular support would have to jettison both idealistic principles, 'however pure', and romantic policies, however high-minded. That Lalor focused on the land as a bread-and-butter issue is not surprising. But he clearly expected leadership to come from higher up the rural ladder than from among the small occupiers of ten acres or less. 'It is never the mass of a people that forms its real and efficient might', he wrote in his final article in the *Felon*,

> It is the men by whom that mass is moved and managed. All the great acts of history have been done by a very few men. Take half a dozen names out of any revolution upon record, and what would have been the result?[67]

Leaders were of more importance than 'the mass of the people'. The latter could furnish everything requisite among the *led:* 'the numbers, the physical strength, the animal daring, the health, hardihood, and endurance'. 'We want only competent leaders', he declared, and if he was unclear whence they might spring, he was certain they would not emerge from among 'the common labourers unable to read and write'. 'It is not the *common* labour, but the *skilled* labour, we desire to engage and organise in this club', he wrote in the *Felon* in July 1848.[68] Clearly, he was as élitist on this point as were other Young Irelanders and/or Confederationists. Having divided the people into the politically articulate and inarticulate, he implied it was incumbent on the former to lead and on the latter to follow. This suggests that he believed rural leadership could only come from those 'independent farmers' (or 'gentlemen farmers') who were attuned to the needs of 'the masses of the people', who were altruistic enough to put tenant interests before class or personal interests, and who nevertheless were not tied to the coat tails of the aristocracy. This is extrememly close to his father's implied case for a new patron/client relationship between middlemen and small holders, as opposed to the prevailing system of general dependence on the aristocracy.

Despite such affinities with his contemporaries, and with his father, it is important to stress that Fintan Lalor used class terminology more often and, in general, with more consistency and clarity than did any of his peers or elders. For him there was no overlapping (and hence no fundamental ambiguity) in the use of such terms as 'order' and 'class'. Though he *did* use the old vocabulary of 'ranks' and 'orders', he did so *only* when attacking the aristocracy's claims to 'lord it' over everyone else; and he used the terminology of 'class', as he had used the legal lexicon — as a lever to oust the aristocracy from their positions of control in all areas of Irish life.

4

Lalor's Economic 'Theories'

(i) LAND, LAW AND THE ECONOMY

Classical economics was 'political' because it concerned itself primarily with the 'ways in which the policies of the state in matters involving trade, manufacture, agriculture, and taxation could be so conducted as to augment the wealth of the sovereign and his subjects'.[1] Despite the rise of *laissez faire* and its avowed faith in the 'invisible hand' regulating the market, economic theorists did not dispense with those 'policies of the state' which made economics (scientific or otherwise) a tool of politics or, more precisely, of power. For Ricardo, Malthus, McCulloch and Mill economics remained 'political'[2] because it was for them, as it had been for Adam Smith, 'a branch of the science of the statesman or legislator'.[3] It, therefore, was not an autonomous discipline in any realistic sense in this period. Locke's doctrine on the relative rights of 'land' and 'labour' as creators of private property[4] provided the vocabulary and the central dilemmas from which the classical economists' later concern with labour and other theories of value emanated.[5] Property, not economics, was the root of the problem and property remained the preserve of jurists well into the nineteenth century. It is, therefore, not surprising that all schemes for improved conditions in Ireland in this period became, in the final analysis, appeals to the State.

As the crux of the problem was undoubtedly the landlord/tenant question, solutions tended to be partisan: either the landlords or the tenants would have to go. 'The two deficiencies in Ireland', Trower wrote to Ricardo, 'are *want of capital* and *want of Industy*. By destroying small tenancies you would obtain both'.[6] Ricardo agreed in principle but felt that the aristocracy 'which rules with a rod of Iron',[7] was the cause of Irish oppression and depression. Improvement, in his view, could only follow the removal of that class. The problem therefore was a legal one: 'If Ireland had a good system of law — if property was secure', he declared, 'capital would flow into Ireland, and . . . would lead to all the beneficial results which everywhere follows from it'.[8] Paradoxically, many of those who agreed with Trower argued on Ricardian grounds that, either the landlords would have to be shown the error of their ways and induced to plough capital and energy into their estates, or they would have to be bought out and replaced by commercially-motivated, capitalist entrepreneurs. The former argument castigated Irish landlords for not following the wise example of their English counterparts; for instead of investing in the land they were a drain on its resources, and as many of them were also absentees their social sins were therby compounded. Not only were they (allegedly) draining capital out of Ireland but they were, by their absence, destroying 'that wholesome dependence of the lower upon the upper classes, which is one of the master links of society'.[9] However, landlords could only improve estates by undertaking massive clearances; which (given the lack of native industrial centres capable of absorbing the dispossessed) implied enormous social dislocation; and this, in turn, raised the temperature of anti-aristocratic feeling. Nassau Senior noted, and denounced as misguided, the inconsistency of those who 'execrate the landlord for his harshness if he be vigilant, and for the wretchedness of his tenants if he be careless'.[10]

Malthusians argued that the pressure on exisitng resources was so great that the only feasible solution was to siphon off the discontented and insecure peasants by promoting mass emigration. The problem therefore was how to induce the peasants to leave. If the bulk of the rural population (and, by implication, of the total population) were hard pressed to find the means of day-to-day subsistence, how could they be expected to scrape together the wherewithal to emigrate? Individual landlords might — and, indeed, some did — *pay* their tenants to leave, but this was a costly procedure and not likely to find many sponsors.[11] Alternative schemes were, of course, proposed. Land, some sophists seemed to say, was not the inelastic commodity which economists would have everyone believe. Marginal or unimproved lands could be brought into cultivation. Indeed, the existence of some 6,205,735 acres of uncultivated ground was often quoted as incontrovertible evidence of the need for an 'improved' agriculture, and was occasionally used as conclusive proof that the population was guilty, not of a too-rapid increase but, of under-utilising Irish land. This view had many sponsors none of whom, it seems, personally tried the experiment of 'farming' the rocky wastes of south west Cork or south Kerry. Robert Kane, who thought height above sea level a definition of waste, asserted:

> there is no district in Ireland sufficiently elevated to thereby present serious impediments to cultivation, and scarcely an acre to which the name of incapable of cultivation can be applied. It has been calculated that of the land at present waste, 4,600,00 acres are really available for agriculture, and from my own investigations, I am inclined to consider that estimate as certainly not exaggerated.[12]

Kane did not feel that 'destitute of agricultural experience, as I have no hesitation to own myself',[13] his opinions were any the less correct. 'Draining', 'reclamation' and 'improvements' (though mere wishful thinking rather than realistic policy) were seriously expected to conjure up out of the bogs of Ireland the new Garden of Eden.

If for the majority of observers the peasant was, as Mansergh succinctly put it, 'an incubus to be removed in the interests of better economics',[14] there was nonetheless a substantial and growing body of pamphleteers and supporters of the smaller tenants. Crawford's hopes for the legalisation of the Ulster Custom, and William Conner's arguments for an independent valuation and a perpetuity for the tenant, were amongst the earliest proposals which favoured the small holders. These activists received additional support from an unexpected quarter in 1848 when John Stuart Mill wrote in the *Morning Chronicle:* 'the people are there, and the problem is not how to improve the country, but how it can be improved *by and for its present inhabitants'*.[15] Both Mill and William Thornton[16] felt that peasant proprietorship was the answer but, as Collison Black remarks, 'both saw that legislation on such lines was not a practical possibility for Ireland in 1848'.[17] Only Lalor — paradoxically, given his involved legal arguments — forwarded a theory which did not depend on State or legislative action.

(ii) LALOR'S ECONOMIC 'THEORIES'[18]

The primary sources of Lalor's later theories would seem to have been the course of study available at Carlow College in 'Political Economy, the Elements of Law in general and in particular the Laws and Constitutions of this Country',[19] and the ideas of his early mentor and fellow-activist William Conner the (self-professed) 'farmer's friend'. Described as being 'a crank of the first water' who was 'intolerant of the opinions of others',[20]

Conner believed that rack-rents were 'the one great cause of all [Ireland's] evils'.[21] He proposed, as the only feasible solution, 'a valuation and perpetuity of his farm to the tenant'.[22] Conner's influence on Lalor is extremely hard to gauge. However, it seems more reasonable to consider their alliance as being less a marriage of true minds than one of convenience. Lalor was far from believing that rack-rents alone were the sum total of the political economy of Ireland, nor did he share Conner's faith in independent valuation and perpetuity as the best means of redress. In any event, the combination of law and economics was a notable feature of Lalor's later writings, and one which would suggest that Conner and he had no more in common than a penchant for Blackstone and a desire to improve the lot of the small-holders. Beyond this they differed greatly, not only in their respective manners of arguing but in their projected means of redress.

Despite the combined influence of Carlow College and of Conner, however, economics for Lalor was not a 'political' but a 'social' matter. He constantly alludes to the need for 'a solid *social* economy' and attempts to outline the means whereby 'the formation of a new *social* economy' might contribute to eradicating the vices of the existing 'political and social' situation. In the contexts in which these phrases occur (in his letters to *The Nation* in 1847) Lalor uses three key, interrelated terms: 'political constitution', 'social constitution', and 'social economy'. However, despite their apparent similarity, these terms refer to analytically discrete areas. Thus, 'social constitution' is the antonym of 'political constitution' — the latter being concerned largely (if not exclusively) with law and institutionalised political power; whereas the former is essentially a matter of national class contours, of the real and discernible face of society. 'Social economy', on the other hand, refers to the particular economic system which a given society (or 'social constitution') creates in order to meet its needs. However, the social aspect of the equation is, for Lalor, more important than the economic. If an economy is in a state of collapse, as was the case in Ireland during the famine, this is due to certain inherent imbalances in the 'social constitution'. Therefore, Lalor argued, ousting the aristocracy would transform the 'social constitution' and would lead, by a natural process (i.e., land redistribution) to an improved 'social economy'. Aristocratic lands being forfeit to 'the people', the small occupiers would not only have absolute ownership of their original plots, but would also have them augmented by the redistribution of aristocratic estates.[23] What, then, would become of rents? The people of Ireland 'in association assembled' would decide 'what rents they [would] pay, and to *whom* they [would] pay them'.[24] Lalor recommended, however,

> that the people on grounds of *policy* and *economy,* ought to decide (as a general rule, admitting of reservations) that those rents shall be paid *to themselves,* the people, for public purposes, and for behoof and benefit of them, the entire general people.[25]

The State or some central agency, it seems clear, would take over the role of landlordism. The monies thus collected would be used in the interests of 'the entire general people' instead of, as heretofore, in the interests of a 'class' of 8,000 aristocrats. Though administration of such a fund — no matter how diminished by the rent-level decided on by the people 'in association assembled'[26] — would be political dynamite for any future central agency or government, this does not worry Lalor unduly; for, in the predominantly agricultural society which he envisaged, the peasantry would have a basic democratic control (some might say stranglehold) on a fundamental lever of possible oppression. That 'the people in association assembled' will vote for an equal redistribution of the land is inevitable, he believes, because when the settlement and law of landed property 'is made by agreement there will be equality of distribution; which equality . . . will remain permanent within certain limits. For under natural laws, landed property has rather a tendency to divide than accumulate.'[27] The implications of this statement are far more important than the presumed role of the State in Lalor's projected scheme. For, if the natural tendency of landed property is towards subdivision rather than consolidation in a few (or a few thousand) hands, what guarantee is there that the expected redistribution of property will not come to grief on the rocks of a future more devastating famine; a famine for which aristocratic or English-government scapegoats would not be available? The answer is tantalisingly simple. Simple because Lalor's basic theory is developmental. Tantalising because its basic mechanism, not to mention its ramifications, are not fully thought out.

Land redistribution will naturally, in Lalor's scheme, lead to industrialisation. In his first letter to *The Nation* he declared that his general object was:

> To organise a new mode and condition of labour — a new industrial system; to frame and fix a new order of society; in a word, to give Ireland a new social constitution under which the natural capacity of the country would be put into effective action; the resources of its land, labour and capital developed and made available; its slumbering and decaying energies of mind and muscle excited, directed and

employed; and the condition and character of its people reconstructed, improved and elevated.[28]

The problem being how 'to create a complete and efficient industrial economy . . . to organise and animate, and put into healthy vigorous action that complex living machine, a social system',[29] Lalor proposed a solution based entirely on agriculture, or (more precisely) on the creation of a strong peasant base to the social fabric. 'Lay the foundation', he advised,

Lay deep and strong the only foundation that is firm under the foot of a nation — a secure and independent agricultural peasantry. A secure and independent agricultural peasantry is the only base on which a people ever rises, or ever can be raised; or on which a nation can safely rest.[30]

Having done this the rest would automatically follow as part of a natural process of organic growth. Nature was the mechanism on which he relied absolutely for the realisation of his 'new industrial system'. Under any other conditions he believed the creation of a social system to be:

A work impossible to man . . . A work of which the theory and the principles are beyond his knowledge or discovery and the practical execution beyond his utmost power. Nature has reserved it to herself, to effect by a process of her own, for which no artificial process was or can be substituted with success. A work we cannot do, God's hand alone, not man's, can do it. True — and neither can you form in all its parts the smallest plant that grows. The powers of vitality but require to be set in movement, and the contrivances of nature left free to act.[31]

From the humble seed of an independent peasantry would blossom, as mysteriously as a flower, the 'new industrial system' of the future. To ask 'how?' is, in Lalor's eyes, to miss the point of the exercise. Suffice it that it works. However, in a long and sometimes repetitive passage which merits quotation *in extenso,*[32] he obliges us with a descriptive account of its growth, and of the stages by which it acquires its industrial petals.

A productive and prosperous husbandry is the sole groundwork of a solid social economy. On it and out of it springs the mechanic, and artisan, and trading dealer; fed and fostered by it these swell into the manufacturer and merchant, who multiply into merchants and manufacturers; sustained by it still, these enlarge, and gather, and solidify into companies, corporations, classes — into great manufacturing and mercantile systems and interests, which often, like unnatural children, disown and desert the mother that bore and the nurse that fed them; without it there is neither manufacture or trade — nor means to make them, for it is agriculture alone that furnishes those means. Food is our first want — to procure it our first work. The agricultural class, therefore, must precede and provide for every other. It is first in order of nature, necessity, and time. It is an abundant agriculture alone that creates and sustains manufactures, and arts, and traffic. It is an increasing agriculture alone that extends them. For it is the surplus of food it accumulates, after providing ordinary subsistence, that forms new wants and demands, and the modes and the means to meet and satisfy them. Such is the actual process; a process that never yet was reversed, or carried out in any other course or order; so it was at first, and so it will be for ever — in every time, in every clime, in every country. Adopt this process; create what has never yet existed in Ireland an active and affluent husbandry, a secure and independent agricultural peasantry, able to accumulate as well as produce — do this and you raise a thriving and happy community, a solid social economy, a prosperous people, an effective nation. Create the husbandman, and you create the mechanic, the artisan, the manufacturer, the merchant. Thus you will work on the ordinance of God, in the order and with the powers of nature. All the natural motives and means with which man is endowed will come then to your relief and assistance, and do the rest. Any further interference with the course and process of natural laws would be useless and mischievous. Neither monarchs nor mobs every yet were able to manage or modify that natural process with success; or ever attempted to enforce interference without doing grievous injury and gross injustice. The abortive and mischievous legislation of both old and recent times affords lessons enough of this, if we choose to learn them.

There seems to be a vague impression on a large portion of the public mind of this country that national attention and exertion, as well as individual effort, should be directed into a course the reverse in its steps and stages of that natural order which I have pointed out. We are in the habit of hearing it asserted that a large development of manufacturing industry is what Ireland needs, and that to establish it should be her chief object. It is even assumed, not unfrequently, that a manufacturing system must precede, and is the only mode of promoting, the improvement and prosperity of agriculture itself. This is an error I could wish to see abandoned. It distracts effort and attention from the point on which both ought to be directed, and on which they could act with effect. I am prepared to prove — what, indeed, any man may prove to himself — that neither by the private enterprise of individuals or companies, neither by the force of national feeling anyhow exerted, neither by public association or public action of any kind or extent nor by government aid, if such aid could be expected — neither by these or any other means and appliances can a manufacturing system be established in Ireland, nor so much as a factory built on firm ground, until the support of a numerous and efficient agricultural yeomanry be first secured. Good friends, you that are recommending us to encourage native manufacture and to form manufacturing associations; tradesmen and townsfolk of Ireland will you cease to follow a phantom, and give hand and help to create such a yeomanry?[33]

Though Lalor's developmental theory *seems* clear enough, it does have a number of inconsistencies. It is true that production of food surpluses is essential for any community in order that the defence forces and government officials (to name but the most strategic groups) may continue to function. It is not self-evident, however, that the peasant-proprietor system which Lalor's land redistribution would create, would be able to produce that surplus. If the 8,000 aristocrats at the apex of the rural social ladder were dispossessed some 13,464,300 acres would be divided up among the 761,695 existing occupiers (assuming, that is, that the agricultural labourers and those holding under one acre would be excluded).[34] The result, if equitable distribution were the order of the day, would be an average holding of 17.68 acres. Given that Lalor believes subdivision to be the natural tendency over time, grossly uneconomical holdings would soon proliferate. How this could lead to anything but subsistence agriculture — by definition unable to accumulate surpluses for the urban sector — is not elucidated, is not even recognised as a problem by Lalor. To further complicate the matter, no indication is given as to whether 'the occupying tenants' (in whom the aristocratic lands are to be vested) refers to direct tenants or to sub-tenants holding from middlemen. If direct tenants are to 'own' the lands which they rent from aristocrats, what is to happen to those sub-tenants who hold directly from rentier middlemen? On the basis of the information which Lalor supplies no realistic answers can be given to these questions. What is most damaging to his case, however, is the fact that he does not at any stage indicate that he realises the existence of such problems.

It should also be noted, that the 'secure and independent agricultural *peasantry*', first presented as the vital basic seed of social and economic reconstruction, inexplicably becomes in the course of his argument 'a numerous and efficient agricultural *yeomanry*'.[35] It is not a simple matter of the former being transformed by economic development into the latter, for Lalor treats both as synonyms. That is, both are seen at different points in the argument as the seed necessary for regeneration. A peasantry, suffice it to say, is *not* a yeomanry.

Finally, we may note the explicit *laissez-faire* attitude to the government's role either in creating industry or in interfering in the natural developmental cycle. To interfere with the process would be 'useless and mischievous'; to finance it using 'government aid' would not even lead to 'so much as a factory built on firm ground'. This attitude is, of course, a product of the popular (and professional) ideological blinkers of the age. The legislature, it was argued, should not interfere in the self-regulating economy as this could disrupt the fragile equilibrium of the market. Like his father before him, Fintan rigidly excluded the State as an economic agent by uncritically accepting the non-interference arguments of the classical economists.

Given Young Ireland's vitriolic hatred of the prevalent Utilitarian doctrine, and its open scorn for English industrialisation as it developed in the early nineteenth century, Lalor's modernisation scheme is intriguing. Despite his reservations about the 'great manufacturing and mercantile systems and interests, which often, like unnatural children, disown and desert the mother that bore and the nurse that fed them',[36] he nonetheless foresees the creation of an industrial system as the inevitable, *and desirable,* end-product of his developmental model. In an earlier draft of this letter, written in 1844, Lalor had shared Young Ireland's disdain for:

> that vile and vicious political philosophy which looks alone to public wealth — to money and the things which are bought with money, without reference or regard to other things of higher account in the true economy of states, than even wealth.[37]

Within three years Lalor seems to have overcome those scruples which earlier had urged him to castigate the English manufacturing system as being, 'when analysed and examined in detail', anything but 'a gratifying subject of contemplation, whether as regards moral or material results.[38] His concluding sarcastic remarks in 1844 indicate how completely his style, but how little his ideas, had changed in the intervening years:

> that England shall manufacture everything (except corn) for the whole world, and shall continue to do so for ever; that no other country shall ever manufacture anything even for itself, that their present markets shall be retained and new markets created, at any expense of blood and treasure, of national justice, or of public morality, colonies founded, defended and kept — with their consent or against their will — armies kept up, navies kept up, and the sword used without scruple or stint, whenever it may be necessary to gain a market or to defend a market. Such are the constant demands of the manufacturing system and I do not wish to say that they are otherwise than most moderate and modest and reasonable.[39]

Even at this early juncture Lalor is not anti-industrial in any meaningful sense. Despite his reservations (and he retains those in 1847), the main thrust of his argument is against English *monopoly* and the means whereby it is defended; *not* against industrialisation *per se.* By 1847 it was more feasible to openly favor the creation of a manufacturing system in Ireland. Robert Kane's *The industrial resources of Ireland* (first published in 1844), was but one of a variety of published lectures which aimed to apply economic principles in order, as he says, 'to correct the exaggerated ideas usually entertained of the disadvantages under which this country labours, in regard to mechanical industry'.[40] However, prevailing views on the topic, including those of the Young Irelanders, centered (perhaps inevitably given their political concerns) on protectionism.[41] The Union, of course, was identified as the prime cause of industrial underdevelopment. It led, so the argument ran, to 'aristocratic extortion' and 'foreign taxation', both of which siphoned capital out of Ireland. Repeal would reverse that process. An Irish parliament in College Green would, it was confidently asserted, 'create vast manufactures . . . by protecting duties in the first instance and . . . [would] maintain them by general prosperity' thereafter.[42]

Lalor's scheme does not depend on protection, and contains no reference to the alleged money-drain of absenteeism. The intellectual sources of his ideas are, however, extremely hard to gauge. Developmental typologies of the 'natural', chronological variety which he favoured were not unusual. Blackstone, for instance, in attempting to trace the historical roots of private property, provided *en passant* a 'developmental' theory which began with a hunter-gatherer stage and led by degrees to the establishment of agricultural settlements.[43] Similarly, Kane provided a typology which began with man's 'first escape from barbarism' and ended with a mutual interdependence between agriculture and industy.[44] While there was considerable variety to such models, most could be reduced to Adam Smith's four states: 'hunting, pasturage, farming and commerce'.[45]

Lalor's scheme, however, has an additional and more concrete aspect based, it seems, on the paths already traversed by France and England. By establishing a peasantry 'rooted like rocks in the soil' he apparently hoped to duplicate the *social* aspects of the French Revolution (1789). In his eyes that revolution 'took France to the sun — gave her wealth, and victory, and renown — a free people and a firm peasantry, lords of their own land'.[46] By a natural process, a similar peasant sector in Ireland would, if created, eventually (though inexplicably) be transformed into an agricultural yeomanry. As the latter was not only an English term but an English phenomenon, it would appear that Lalor envisaged for Ireland a landed regime similar to that which had existed during the period of industrialisation in England. The steps, therefore, were: the creation of a native and secure peasantry which would, in time, develop into an 'agricultural yeomanry' leading in turn to the emergence of a manufacturing system.

On examination, the scheme reveals many weaknesses. Firstly, it overestimates the effects of the Revolution on land-holding in France: according to one student, 'the sales of confiscated lands and voluntary sales, [effected] primarily a transfer of property *within the upper classes*. Basically the existing agrarian structure was consolidated'.[47] In addition, it was not (and is not) feasible to institute *general* comparisons between Irish and French peasant conditions. Climatic and geographical factors created considerable local variations throughout France. Hence, the peasantry of the south, working in a Mediterranean climate and subject to the land uses which it made possible, differed in numerous respects from their counterparts in the north of France. Lalor's arguments, therefore, would need to specify precisely what area was to be used as a model for the future development of the Irish peasant sector. Even at the most general level any comparison would need to take into account the fact that whilst the Irish peasant economy was essentially a subsistence monoculture, that of France was a subsistence *poly*culture.[48] As for the creation of an agricultural yeomanry, the evidence suggests that they were created on the ruins of the peasantry and not (as Lalor seems to imply) by a natural evolution from that sector.[49]

In spite of these criticisms Lalor's theory is important. Both in his attitude and in his terminology he is at variance with the Confederation and Young Ireland, and is certainly unique within his circle. His vocabularly contains both orthodox terms — such as 'land', 'labour' and 'capital' — and seemingly idiosyncratic neologisms — such as 'overplus' (for 'surplus') and 'social economy' (instead of the more common 'political economy'). Whilst it is true that Isaac Butt and John Stuart Mill both employed the phrase 'social economy',[50] Lalor's use of the term pre-dates both of theirs. It may, in fact, have been a peculiarly Lalorite coinage though this seems doubtful.[51] It certainly had a very specific meaning in his scheme and was closely intertwined with his use of such related phrases as 'social constitution' and 'political constitution'. Where Lalor's intellectual or theoretical roots actually lie is not easy to discern. It should be noted, however, that there is nothing in his model which would indicate that he had been influenced by Friedrich List's *National system of political economy*, which first appeared in English translation in 1841.[52] Specifically, Lalor did not argue for a *national* system of *political* economy, nor did he advocate protection in order to foster home industry. In addition, he shared neither List's unalloyed enthusiasm for the industrial system, nor his arguments relegating agriculture to a subservient role in the total economy.[53]

Where Lalor's *particular* intellectual debts may lie, (especially in matters of economic theory), it is impossible to say with any certainty at this juncture. However, it seems clear that, *in general*, (i.e., in matters of approach and emphasis) he was influenced less by the classical economists than by the French physiocrats of the late-eighteenth century. Like them, he based his theories on the belief that 'Human society . . . was ruled by natural laws which could never be altered by the positive laws of statecraft'.[54] Like them, he stressed the primary role of agricultural surpluses in generating further economic growth. Like them, he assumed that the non-agricultural sectors of an agrarian economy (in this case that of Ireland) would 'naturally' grow 'in sympathy with, and in response to, the growth of the agricultural sector'. And, like them, he believed that this economic growth was inevitable — provided only that 'governmental intervention, . . . special privilege and monopoly, and . . . other interferences with the competitive process' were rigorously disallowed.[55]

In most respects, these tenets were indistinguishable from those of classical economics. (*Laissez faire,* after all, was originally a *physiocratic* slogan). However, given that classical economic orthodoxies have often, correctly, been charged with exacerbating (if not causing) the great famine, it remains to be seen how Lalor, as a latter-day physiocrat, viewed that catastrophe and how he proposed to deal with it.

(iii) LALOR'S VIEW OF THE FAMINE

I have just seen in the *Nation* of last Saturday, May 1, . . . [an] extract from the lecture of Dr Hughes on the 'Condition of Ireland'.

Doctor Hughes does not seem sufficiently to understand how the failure of a single root can have produced a famine. "The vice of our political and social economy is one that eludes inquiry." But is it indeed so obscure? Has it then been able to conceal or disguise itself? It must be dragged out. In self-defence the question is now forced on us, whether there be any particular class or institution specially chargeable?[56]

Lalor's question contains the seeds of his eventual answer. In his eyes the aristocracy were not only 'considered chargeable with the calamitous crisis that has occurred',[57] but were at fault also 'for assisting the natural operation of the famine instead of arresting it — putting the tenant out of his foothold of land instead of aiding him to retain and cultivate it.[58] Implicit in his attack on the 'particular class' of 8,000 aristocrats was the assumption that *they* were not seriously affected by the famine; that, as landlords, they could have afforded to forego their rent-collecting labours until the crisis had passed. For this reason, their (assumed) lucrative position at the apex of the social and economic ladder prompted not analysis but condemnation. The picture that Lalor paints of 'the natural operation of the famine' is, consequently, biased and demands careful treatment. This is not to suggest that his alarm and indignation were either unusual or, in themselves, less than commendable. Quite the opposite in fact. Exasperation, frustration and despair were shared features of all accounts of the calamity, from Butt's relatively sober article[59] to the *Nation's* hysterical outbursts. 'What is to be done?', that journal asked in January 1847.

Such is the startling, the appalling question which every lover of his country asks himself, and which every thinker is striving to answer; and rapidly it is becoming still more appalling, still more startling. Scarcity has ripened into famine, and disease and crime are stalking in its footprints. Every day's account is big with misery, and scenes of woe at which the heart sickens are in thousands of habitations. What is to be done? Alas! Alas! our greatest calamity is that we can do nothing.[60]

Isaac Butt was less supine when he echoed the question four months later. 'No more profitable investment for state expenditure than Ireland now presents, was ever offered to the exchequer of a great nation', he asserted.[61] To meet the crisis he proposed a basket of measures ranging from railway construction and emigration (an unusual combination in which, presumably, the railroads would hasten the journey to the dockside) to the reclamation and colonisation of wasteland. His confidence in such measures alone was, however, less than absolute:

Never was there an occasion [his analysis concluded] upon which it was more fitting, that our Sovereign and her people should bow in submission to the mysterious will of the Great Being who rules us all — and earnestly implore his mercy for a suffering land; and that blessing, without which the wisest of human legislation is in vain.[62]

The magnitude and complexity of the problem seemed to defy analysis and/or solution. It is, perhaps, not surprising therefore that some commentators thought they discerned particular institutions or classes which they believed were more culpable than others. Mitchel, for example, provided one of the most enduring maxims of the century when he wrote: 'The Almighty, indeed, sent the potato blight, but the English created the famine'.[63] Lalor's scapegoat was closer to home: though he agreed that the blight was 'a visitation of God, in the order of nature', the landlords, he believed, made the famine.

He proves their ultimate responsibility for the crisis by sketching the natural, day-to-day conditions of both the labourers and the small holders on the eve of blight. The independent labourer 'depending altogether on wages for subsistence' could not find constant employment throughout the year. In order to feed himself and his family, therefore, he took a quarter of an acre of conacre land at £2-12s-6d for six months (1 May to 1 November). The land was manured by the farmer by Devonshiring; that is by paring off the top-soil, burning it and scattering it over the quarter acre. Thus manured — 'for in no other mode was it ever manured' — the labourer planted potatoes. When the time came to dig them, however, 'there were none to be digged. Two hundred and thirty thousand families began to die of hunger; and famine ran wild into fever.'[64]

Similarly, the small holders — those in occupation of 'farms' of ten acres or less — depended on potatoes for subsistence. 'This class of men', Lalor asserts, 'differed little in the appearance, but very much in the reality of circumstance and condition, from the class of men labourers'. Those holding five acres or less, and particularly those on the one acre margin, were 'labourers with allotments'. They enjoyed more security and status than the labourers but, nevertheless, shared the same hand-to-mouth existence. These, the smallest holdings, were almost entirely in tillage. Corn was raised to pay the rent, and potatoes to feed the family. Where the grain crop was insufficient to meet the rent of the holding, a pig was also kept.[65]

One rung above these were the families in occupation of farms varying in size from five to ten acres 'but none of them exceeding that extent'. Those on the ten acre margin had a portion of land in pasture, but depended largely, like those beneath them, on a corn/potato system for rent and food. At this level of holding a hog fed on potatoes might go to procure 'mere luxuries such as shoes, wearing apparel, and other articles of convenience'.[66] The larger the holding the greater the relative financial security. However, all holdings of ten acres or under were held, Lalor asserts, 'by no other assurance, legal or moral, than [the] landlords' pecuniary personal interest in retaining [them] as tenants'.[67] Thus, when famine came, the landlord took the corn crop and the tenants starved. There were, of course, 'petty exceptions':

> in districts of Tipperary the tenants, or many of them, kept their corn for food — thus paying themselves for their labour, capital, and seed, and saving their own lives — instead of paying the rent. It may be said that in those districts the full rents were not paid; it may be said that in Galway, Mayo, Cork, and elsewhere they *could not* be paid. The oat crop failed partially, as the potato failed wholly.[68]

Despite these exceptions, Lalor asserts that 'the landlords took entire possession of last year's harvest — of the whole effective sum and substance of that harvest'[69] and the tenants, left without seed or substance, starved. Relief committees, depending on landlord alms, were insufficient to meet the crisis. Given that the landlords' aim was to consolidate their holdings by clearing their estates of the small holders, they were, thereby, assisting the 'natural operation of the famine'. They 'demanded the Labour Rates Act' in order to spur those starving on the land to give up their meagre plots, and throw themselves on the mercy of the relief system. While 'the lord of the soil got his rent and became a public and professed patriot', the small-holding tenants were deprived of food or the means to grow it.

The tenant had neither seed nor subsistence; or, if he had any small provision of either, he was soon deprived of it by the relief system. Whatever seed he might have saved from the landlord; whatever little means he possessed for making manure; whatever small capital was in his hands to work with, were taken from him by relief committees and relieving officers. The law was laid down, and acted on very generally, that no man should obtain either gratuitous relief or public employment until he should first be completely pauperised. If he had seed corn, he should consume it, if he had a cow he should sell it — and not a few of them said, as they are still saying, 'if he had land he should give it up'; otherwise they could have no title to relief.[70]

In this way the blight was being assisted in its course, and famine was being used as a cloak for the active policy of clearance. The small holders, those in occupation of ten acres or less, were being converted into 'independent labourers' and the landlords, Lalor alleged, were assisting the process by evictions, compulsory surrenders and forced sales. Without even marginally treating or attempting to understand the landlords' position, Lalor attacks them in no uncertain terms as the villains of the piece. His attitude, it would seem, is based less on an impartial and knowledgeable assessment of famine conditions throughout Ireland, than on his disdain for the local aristocrat Sir Charles Henry Coote, the largest landholder in County Laois.[71]

In March 1847, roughly a week before he wrote the above details for *The Nation*, Lalor wrote to D'Arcy McGee explaining his principles:

Do you [he asked] assent to my principle in its full integrity of ownership of the land as well as legislation? Your reason may assent, yet your feelings revolt. Now listen. There was in Ireland in 1647 a certain Sir Charles Coote. He bought lands in Ireland and paid for them too with lead and steel. There is now in this country in 1847 another Sir Charles Coote, his lineal descendant, who holds his lands and stands in his shoes — whether or not he treads in his footsteps. His rents are beyond £40,000 a year. The tenantry of his many estates throughout the county paid up their rents last November, were forced to pay them, and are now famishing to death. To the Relief Fund of the parish he resides in, he gave thirty pounds — one sixth per cent of his annual income. To no other parish did he give one penny though his estates are everywhere.[72]

Within a week this attack on Coote was incorporated into an abstract attack on *all* aristocrats. As a result of the famine, he wrote:

The landowners grew bustling, if not busy, in the work of demanding relief and dispensing it. To the local relief funds very many of them, indeed, contributed even so large a sum as 000.0001/4 per cent of their annual income, and were most properly appreciated and praised as beneficent individuals.[73]

Clearly, his disdain for Coote is at the core of his attck on the aristocracy. Hence, his view of the famine is suspect. Whilst his sketch of the conditions under which 'independent labourers' and small-holders existed is correct in its outlines and is corroborated by much contemporary evidence,[74] there is little that would prove that he had an extensive knowledge of conditions outside Laois, Kildare, Tipperary, and parts of Cork, Limerick and Carlow. Particular aspects of his treatment, in fact, strongly suggest that his knowledge was based almost entirely on local conditions in County Laois. For instance, insofar as it was true at all, his assertion that the labourer 'depended altogether on wages for subsistence' had, perhaps, more relevance for the east than for the west coast. Proximity to Dublin and to the English market, possibly meant that the monetary economy had relatively deeper roots there than in other parts of Ireland. Whether or not this was so, labourers in other areas more often than not paid their dues in service or kind, and were paid in the same manner by those who employed them. Money was seldom used in such transactions anywhere in Ireland. Nonetheless, the evidence suggests that there existed a declining spectrum of monetisation which had its geographical termini in Ulster and the Dublin hinterland (at its apex), and in the extreme south and west (at its nadir). Granted there were pockets of monetisation throughout the rural economy; but the increasing prevalence of conacre farming and the proportionate increase in the number of extremely small holdings, suggests that money was less a medium of exchange or a unit of account in the west and south-west, than in the north and east.[75]

In addition, Lalor's allegation that conacre land was let at a rate of £2-12s-6d the quarter acre for six months (ten guineas per acre the half-year), does not take into account the fact that there were considerable fluctuations from county to county. In Cavan and Fermanagh, for instance, manured land was let at £8 per acre; in Down, 'from £8 to £12 the Irish acre'; in Clare, 'from £3-10s to £8 per Irish acre'; in Cork, 'from £4 to £7, according to the quality; it seldom exceeds £7'; in Kerry for £4 or £5 an acre; in Limerick, 'from 4s to £1 per quarter of an acre (Irish measure)'; in Tipperary, 'from £8 to £14. I have known it', one witness claimed, '[to be] as high as £14' for burned land; in Kilkenny, Carlow, Dublin, Queen's (Laois), and Wicklow it varied from £6 to £12 per acre, the most common rate (depending on land-quality and crop) being £8 to £10. In Galway, Mayo, Leitrim, Roscommon, and Sligo it varied from £6 to £10 for burnbate ground, generally being highest in the vicinity of towns.[76] Lalor's figures, therefore, are far from representative.

Nor is he entirely correct in asserting that Devonshiring, or burnbate, was the sole (because traditional) way in which conacre land was manured. Practices varied depending on the crop and on the quality of land taken. Good grassland, for instance, was seldom manured; whilst medium, poor, or very weak soils were as often limed or manured with sea-weed and sand (this being especially prevalent along the west coast) as they were pared and burned.[77]

Lalor's description of the subsistence economy of rural Ireland, therefore, suggests a degree of uniformity which clearly did not exist. That he failed to take into account considerable local variations may, in part, be due to the fact that he was writing to a newspaper. This need not have hampered him unduly had he been willing to undertake a detailed statistical account of prevailing conditions. Francis Dowdall, for instance, published a series of such articles in the *Dublin Evening Herald* in 1846.[78] Lalor's decision to provide a picture of grim uniformity might, therefore, have had other roots. It may, indeed, have been due in large measure to the fact that he was addressing a specific audience: 'The details I am giving', he alleged, 'are sufficiently well known here, but I write for England'.[79] That being the case, he was more likely to write from personal, local experience than from deep or prolonged study of the available data. There is, however, a more important reason for distrusting his arguments. His evidence is seriously undermined by his too obvious concern to make a case for the smallholders (whose conditions — bad as they were, even at the best of times — are, therefore, likely to be presented in as unattractive a light as possible) against the tight-fisted depredations of the aristocracy. That case, however, was not quite as water-tight as he might have hoped. In fact, a little thought suffices to undermine his anti-landlord polemic. Quite apart from the fact that — as was well known even at the time — many landlords were in serious financial straits and could not afford to forego rents from their tenants or sub-tenants, Lalor's argument founders completely on the rocks of contemporary market changes. The confiscations, he asserts,

> will not be limited to ten-acre holdings. There are causes in operation which will render it impossible for tillage to pay as high a rent as land under grass. Many causes — some natural, others artificial — render it impossible to produce corn in this country at as low a cost, quality for quality, as it can be produced in most others. Our corn will soon be undersold in the market by a superior article — a result rendered surer and speedier by the present increased demand for foreign corn. Shortly too, the house-feeding of cattle can no longer be carried on. Even if the repeal of the corn duty should realise the utmost expectations of its advocates, and if there should be, consequently, a proportionate increase in the demand for beef, mutton, butter, and wool, yet the tillage land of Ireland turned into grass land, will be fully adequate to supply the increased demand. House-feeding will be unable to compete against grass-feeding, or to pay for itself. Together with corn, therefore, the root crops will no longer be raised; a regular system of active cultivation is sustained by corn alone. The agriculture that employs and maintains millions will leave the land, and an agriculture that employs only thousands will take its place. Ireland will become a pasture ground once again, as it was before.[80]

The market is undergoing changes which, as Lalor realises, will result in higher rents for pasture ground. Landlords, therefore, in attempting to change over from tillage to pasture, are guilty of nothing more than rational economic behaviour. In addition, with the collapse of the corn/subsistence economy on which small-holders have hitherto relied, it would seem that Lalor's arguments (not only about the nature and effects of the famine, but also concerning his proposed, peasant-based, developmental model) are basically unsound. For instance, the collapse of the corn market implies the destruction of the dual-crop economy on which small-holders have come to rely. Enormous dislocation despite famine conditions, therefore seems inevitable with time. Granted the dislocation caused by changing market demands might be more gradual than that caused by famine; yet it is nonetheless true (and Lalor is aware of it) that clearance is inevitable. This, in turn, implies that the new peasant-based regime which he envisages once the landlords have been ousted, has very shaky foundations. For if the market for corn no longer exists, what security can small-holders have on their farms — even if they own them 'from the sod to the sky'? The trauma of famine has ensured that there can be no large-scale return to the subsistence economy of potato cultivation. As Lalor himself put it:

The potato was our sole and only capital, to live and work on, to make much or little of; and on it the entire social economy of this country was founded, formed and supported. That system and state of things can never again be resumed or restored; not even should the potato return.[81]

In addition, the repeal of the corn laws has robbed the small farmer of a market for his rent crop. As a result, the two-crop economy is in ruins, and there is nothing in Lalor's writings that would suggest he knows of a feasible solution. Even the possibility of small-holders attempting to live on the margins of the pasture economy is unlikely given that, as Lalor admits, 'house-feeding will be unable to compete against grass-feeding, or to pay for itself'. Despite his alarmist reaction to the repeal of the corn laws, and on the basis of the evidence he provides, the conclusion must be that his arguments are untenable. Not only are they an explanation and rationalisation of the landlords' (albeit inhumane) policy, but they also provide the nails for the coffin of his developmental 'model'.

In conclusion, how realistic was Lalor's view of the dual-crop rent/subsistence economy?[82] The evidence suggests that it was a more resilient and entrenched system than he realised. The pre-famine tillage economy hung on desperately until the bad harvests of the early 1860s. However, it had been on the decline since 1851, the year of its maximum post-famine extent. Oats, it is true, reached their peak in 1852 and potatoes in 1859, but grazing was slowly but surely gaining ground in the years after the famine.[83] The decline of tillage was less a reflection of market changes (caused by the repeal of the corn laws) than a direct result of famine. In 1841 almost 45% of all 'farms' were in the one to five acre bracket, and a further 36% ranged from over five to fifteen acres. By 1851 these small holdings were almost entirely obliterated. One to five acre holdings fell from 310,436 in 1841 to 88,083 a decade later; at which point they represented a mere 15% of the total number of holdings. Those in the five to fifteen acre bracket did not fall so far proportionately (36% to 33% approximately) but in absolute terms the decline was still great: from 252,799 in 1841 to 191,854 ten years later.[84] The small holders had been virtually obliterated. Where they survived — along the western seaboard — the pre-famine, dual-crop economy continued in existence.

Population pressure, therefore, explains the continuation of 'traditional' tillage farming despite changed market demands. In fact, the economic motives for change from tillage to pasture had existed since the end of the Napoleonic wars in 1815 but as Crotty shows, falling agricultural prices did not affect the subsistence economy.[85] Short-term resonsiveness to market changes can not easily be assessed for the famine years,[86] especially as the collecting and collating of comprehensive agricultural statistics was not begun until 1847. However, a perusal of the available data makes it clear that there was no panic flight to economic extremes. In 1847 some 3,313,579 statute acres were under corn crops, whilst an additional 284,116 acres were under potatoes.[87] The corn acreage dropped in successive years to reach the three million mark in 1851, by which time potato cultivation accounted for 868,501 acres.[88] Thus, the potato economy on which the majority relied continued in existence despite the drop in corn production. The slump in prices caused by the repeal of the corn laws did not affect the struggle for subsistence. Lalor's alarmist fears about the market had — understandably — no immediate relevance for those whose over-riding aim was to stay alive. Pig exports, for example, though considerably reduced from the panic levels of 1846 (480,827) continued at a high level down to 1851 (68,053) with exports during the intervening years fluctuating around the 100,000 mark.[89]

Connaught — with 43% of the six million acres of uncultivated land in the country, and with the highest proportion of one to five acre holdings — was most dependent on the corn/potato economy. It was the least fertile and the most densely populated province outside Ulster, and Lalor had no acquaintance with its inhabitants or their conditions. In fact, the continued survival of the pre-famine economy in the west, highlights the inaccuracies of his analysis and expectations. Neither the corn laws nor the famine materially changed the nature of Connaught society in the ensuing years. Nor is it immediately self-evident that redistribution of aristocratic land (including some two and a half million acres of waste) and the creation of a strong peasantry 'rooted like rocks' in the rock-filled soil, ever would or could accumulate the supluses necessary for the foundation of 'a new industrial system'.

(iv) CONCLUSIONS

Young Irelanders in general reserved for economic matters, and especially for the industrial economy of England, a moral disdain which precluded any suggestion that Ireland might possibly be improved by grubbing in the Utilitarian till. Not that improvement *per se* was frowned on, but that, in their high-minded, ethical way they feared moral degeneration would result from material advancement. Davis, for instance, was misled by his idealised view of rural Ireland, and his rueful belief that the peasantry were a vanishing breed, into a conviction (as economically spurious as it was ethically pure) that cottage industries and small holdings would improve the Irish economy. Lacking sympathy with the aims and methods of the 'dismal science', and appalled by the immoral results of industrialisation and urbanisation in England, he and his heterogeneous coterie were singularly ill-equipped to pontificate on the means by which the Irish economy would or could be improved.

Alone within this circle, Lalor wrote of industrialisation as an end desirable in itself. Whilst he shared the prevalent moral concern for the degradation engendered in England by the rise of an industrial economy, his attitude was less one of outright condemnation than of envy. He wished to emulate, not eradicate, the English system. The means whereby this would be achieved, the developmental model which he proposed, was clear in its outlines but imprecise in details, and emphasised institutional changes rather than market trends. Specifically, he asserted that the creation of a firm agricultural sector (in which peasants farmed the redistributed lands of a dispossessed aristocracy) would lead in time to a 'solid social economy' and a new 'industrial system'. The peasantry would become a yeomanry, and would (mysteriously) provide the raw material for growth. How this was to be achieved in the face of market changes (caused by the repeal of the corn laws), which he clearly expected would undermine the peasant tillage economy, is not explained. At root, however, his economic 'model' — though certainly unique for his time and circle — was simply an unbridled admixture of anti-landlord polemics and physiocratic policies. By arguing that owner-occupancy would provide the impetus necessary for economic growth, and inferring that landlord rapacity was the only existing bar to the amassing of peasant agricultural surpluses, he championed the cause of the small holders even as he was blaming the aristocracy for the economic collapse!

Whilst Lalor's adaptation and presentation of physiocratic arguments is certainly ingenious, there is nothing to validate the rather generous assertion that his economic expertise was such that he 'might well have directed his efforts to the founding of a school of Political Economy for Small Nations'.[90] His developmental theory was both ingenious and unique, but it had serious flaws. Indeed, it was less a theory than a typology, an outline from which we might extract any amount of possible scenarios; and both the famine and the repeal of the corn laws raised serious doubts about its feasibility.

Finally, it should be noted that, because Lalor saw the causes and consequences of the famine in class-specific rather than national terms, his proposed remedies, also, were class-specific. Thus, he argued that whereas the potato blight was a natural phenomenon, the famine was a product of landlord ineptitude and rapacity. Therefore, to survive the former one ate other foodstuffs; but, to put an end to the famine, one had to put an end to the landlords. Both of these goals could be achieved, he believed, by the simple and economical expedient of withholding rents. This would not only drive the landlords off the land, but would also, simultaneously, make the rent crop available to the tenants as a foodstuff. Thus, his attacks on the aristocracy, pulsing with rhetorical fire, were not (he believed) mere idle exercises in public anger; they were backed up by a very radical, indeed revolutionary, threat.

However, he could not deliver on such a threat. As a general policy for dealing with the calamity of famine, his proposed rent strike suffered from several crippling defects. Its most immediate drawback was that it alienated virtually all potential supporters (especially Young Irelanders) by its impious disregard for the sacred rights of property. In addition, whilst it might have proved adequate to the immediate needs of the one-to-ten acre tenants, (whom Lalor was apt to equate with 'the people') it would not, of itself, have met those of the cottiers and landless labourers, or of the lower classes in the towns and cities. In fact, since withholding rents primarily meant withholding crops rather than money, a rent strike could only be successful if *all* holdings were producing a large enough non-potato rent crop to meet their occupants' food requirements. To assume that this was the case seems, to me, unwarranted — particularly in the case of con-acre and cottier lands. In general, the smaller the holding the less likely it was that suspending or striking against rents would, of itself, meet the crisis caused by the famine. Indeed, it is clear that in Ireland's largely non-monetised, rural economy of the 1840s — based almost exclusively on potato cultivation — no *one* measure would, of itself, have been adequate to the demands of the situation. Given this, and the fact that classical capitalism, though newly-tirumphant in England, had proved incapable of dealing with the vagaries and idiosyncracies of undevelopement in the neighbouring island, we can hardly (reasonably) expect greater success from Lalor's individual, and very local, initiative. However, it might be argued that, under the circumstances, his proposed rent strike (forwarded in early 1847) at least had the virtue of being more humane than anything then being attempted by the English government, or advocated by Irish landlords.

5

Conclusion: Identity and Influence

(i) INTRODUCTION

Aided by a combination of native avarice and British policy making, the famine, (the last great subsistence crisis in Western Europe), effected a revolution in Irish society[1] such as could normally have occurred only after enormous bloodshed and civil strife. Between 1845 and 1851, *at least* 800,000 people died of fever and starvation, and a million more were forced into immediate emigration. These draconian quantitative changes, confined largely to the lower strata of society, were effected with relative ease and led, gradually, to the emergence of a *qualitatively* different society. The virtual disappearance of the marginalised small-holders, and of the dispossessed and despised landless labourers, whose ranks were effectively and ruthlessly decimated by the famine, made possible the emergence of what is now referred to, simply, as 'post famine society'. In contrast to its pre-famine counterpart, this new society was characterised by pasture rather than tillage farming; by unigeniture and consolidated holdings, rather than multiple inheritance and sub-division; by a relatively late age at marriage for both sexes (sometimes amounting to lifelong celibacy), and a consequent decline in the birth rate; and — perhaps most debilitating of all in a country not noted for its natural capital — by a constant stream of socially enforced (as opposed to economically unavoidable) emigration.

If this was not the social landscape that classical economists, government policy makers, Repealers, and Young Irelanders had concretely envisaged when they talked of enforcing law and order, creating an improved agriculture, giving Ireland an independent legislature, and reducing the surplus population, it was nonetheless the one their policies were most likely to produce. In the first half-century of the Union, for instance, Westminster had countered endemic Irish unrest with a continuous and unrelieved litany of coercive legislation. In the same period, domestic political parties, especially Repeal and Young Ireland, had tended to deal with rural distress by taking refuge in an absurd social romanticism. And classical economists, (and others interested in 'the problem' of Ireland), because they were more concerned for the rights of property-owners than for the propertyless, invariably declared that the 'surplus population' should be cleared off the land and spirited away by the panacea of emigration. Thus, in wishing to placate, to 'pacify', rural Ireland, all these agencies and advocates of change (domestic and foreign), were in fact admitting that they were inadequate to the needs of the governed. For they sought, by one means or another, to reduce the population, not employ it; to break its spirit, not channel its energies; to subdue it, rather than govern it.

It was because he realized that the success of such policies was predicated on the destruction of the small-holders that Lalor attempted to rouse them to resistance. He sought to strengthen their case, not only by providing a full battery of legal and economic justifications, but also by seeking political support for his arguments. The urgency of his appeal was magnified by the tragedy of the famine, which, he declared in a letter to the Confederation in early '47, '[is creating] a revolution . . . which will leave Ireland *without a people,* unless it be met and conquered by a revolution which will leave it without landlords'.[2]

Despite his 'passionate persuasive rhetoric', however, Lalor's ideas served but to divide the Confederation, and to prove beyond a doubt that Young Ireland might change its name but was incapable (as a 'party') of changing its political colours. Mere matters of 'class' never quite penetrated their obsession with national identity. If we are Irish, they declared, yet we are loyal to Queen and Empire. If we seek repeal and argue passionately in its favour, we do not, for all that, seek separation. Commonwealth status, as it emerged in the twilight of the Empire, would have answered their arguments and aspirations. The famine, it is true, changed and embittered the minds of some (particularly Mitchel), yet Irish politics returned to Westminster in the 1850s, undeterred by the defeats which it had experienced in that 'gentlemen's club' in the previous decade. The tenor and content of political grievance were changed, however. Its aims were more precise and, perhaps, more prosaic. The repeal sky being no longer the (unattainable) limit, the more mundane bread-and-butter politics of tenant right emerged into the political light of day.

(ii) LALOR'S IDEOLOGICAL 'IDENTITY'

Though Fintan Lalor had done more than most to enable the 'agricultural classes' to find their political voice, he would not have shared the Tenant Right League's confidence in the policy of petitioning Westminster. Such a process, he believed, was foolhardy in the extreme: 'You commit yourselves, in the position of paupers, to the mercy of English ministers and of English members; you throw your very existence on English support'. As a permanent minority, Irish representatives could only become 'a mark for pelting at'.[3] To agitate for Irish reforms in an impervious imperial parliament entailed a respect for political forms which Lalor did not share. 'Political rights', he declared in his first letter to *The Nation,* 'are but paper and parchment'. Fourteen months later, in the first number of the *Felon,* he elaborated considerably on this:

> For let no people deceive themselves, or be deceived by the words and colours, and phrases and forms of a mock freedom, by constitutions, and charters and articles, and franchises. These things are paper and parchment, waste and worthless. Let laws and institutions say what they will, this fact will be stronger than all laws, and prevail against them, the fact that those who own your land will make your laws, and command your liberties and your lives.[4]

The real enemy, therefore, was not the English govenment but the Irish aristocracy, and Lalor aimed to subvert 'the tyranny' of this 'class of 8,000' by attacking its legitimating roots in English law. It is, therefore, putting the cart before the horse to suggest that: 'In his theories on the origins of the rights of property, Lalor was strongly influenced by his application of Irish independence to Blackstone's interpretation of English law.'[5] In fact, independence, as seen by Repealers and Young Irelanders alike, meant nothing to Lalor. Repeal he derided as 'a petty parish question' and 'an impractical absurdity'; and the literary and romantic nationalism of Young Ireland, as enunciated in *The Nation*, he declared 'the mere craving of genius for a *magnificent* subject, instead of a *mean* one'. Such a movement, he wrote, was proof 'that a "glorious agitation" *affords no poetry,* whilst insurrection *does*', and he warned against 'building up or restoring an ideal nationality which time is wearing down, and wasting away, faster than men can work it up'.[6]

He was, thus, by temperament and choice, adrift from the two dominant movements of the decade. His own concern was with social and economic collapse, rather than with possible future forms of government. As he himself put it:

> Eight thousand men are owners of this island . . . claiming the right of enslaving, starving, and exterminating eight millions. We talk of asserting free government, and of ridding ourselves of foreign domination . . . while lo! eight thousand men are lords of our lives . . . of us and ours, blood and breath, happiness and misery, body and soul.[7]

The struggle in which he was engaged, therefore, was not concerned with orthodox political parties (such as the Repeal Association), with political panaceas (independence), or with popular political forms (franchises, charters or parliaments). His aim was, quite simply, to overthrow the aristocracy. To describe him as a 'nationalist', therefore, effectively leaves his central beliefs untouched.

If he was not a nationalist, was he perhaps an anarchist? He believed, as did most libertarians, not only that man is a 'naturally social animal' whose best guide is 'natural law', but also 'that the organisation of community life on a political level should be replaced by its social and economic organisation on the basis of free contractual agreement'.[8] Despite this common ground, however, he was not an anarchist. It is possible to be so definite because his own references to '*social* anarchy' were decidedly negative,[9] and would have horrified most libertarians, given their view that society is a seamless web which mysteriously coheres despite conflict. For them, anarchy was a *political*, not a social condition. It meant, as its Greek root implies, 'a society without government'.[10] Lalor, however, aimed, not to overthrow government *per se*, but to put an end to the aristocratic domination of Irish society. In addition, whereas anarchists viewed the social contract as an 'agreement between individuals', Lalor saw it as an agreement *between classes*.[11]

His use of 'class', it might therefore be contended, if it disqualified him as a libertarian, surely proves he was a socialist? However, given that class terminology was part of the common vocabulary of rhetoric and dispute and was not confined to socialists, his use of 'class' cannot validate such an interpretation. Nor did he advocate (as the traditional interpretation of his alleged socialism implies) either State ownership of, nor a communitarian solution to, the land question. Though aristocratic lands were to be confiscated and redistributed, this would not be done on a communitarian basis, nor would it involve the State as an active landowner or agent. In fact, there is not enough information in his writings for us to be able to treat of his opinions of the State with any confidence. The term occurs only once in his letters, and very little can be hazarded on such a basis. Even were we to equate 'government' with 'State', we would still not have solved the problem; for, Lalor implies that the policy of government is essentially, if not solely, that of *laissez faire.* In fact, he argued, even during the calamity of famine, that government policy should be to remain aloof:

> It is not a case to which governments or parliaments are competent [he declared]. The sole office and duty of government under the circumstances is that of supporting the desitute, and maintaining public order during the period of transition [from the old order to the new]. Should it attempt doing more than this, it will be assuming a power which it does not possess, and cannot even make an effort to exercise without committing injustice, doing injury, and suffering defeat.[12]

This accurately reflects his fundamental belief that in cases of crisis, the individual members (or classes) of society are the only agents capable of effecting any real change. Society, in effect, has to cure itself since government is not competent to act. Whatever else this may be, it is clearly not socialist. The final, and perhaps most damaging, disproof of his alleged socialism, is the evident disdain with which he wrote of the 'common', 'unread', 'mere' labourers. Their condition, more appalling in many respects than that of the small-holders, did not interest him at all.

If he was not a nationalist, nor an anarchist, nor a socialist, *what was he?* E.R. Norman claims that his tenets, being 'at once Lockian and populist', were less an attempt to foster 'rural socialism' than to create 'a sort of Jeffersonian farmers' republic'.[13] Perhaps. But — *what sort?* No doubt Lalor would have shared Jefferson's belief 'that farmers are the best social base of a democratic republic',[14] (though 'republic' was not a term he used).[15] However, he would have scoffed at any one so benighted as to wish 'never . . . to see our citizens occupied at a work bench or twirling a distaff', or so foolhardy as to declare 'Let our workshops remain in Europe'![16] If he supported the primacy of agriculture, he did not, for all that, berate the need for manufactures.

What of Lalor's own claim, in a letter to Peel in 1843, that he was a Conservative? He certainly appealed to the law with all the force and vigour of a Tory. However, whereas Conservatives used an array of legal arguments to support and legitimise the traditional order, Lalor appealed to the same laws precisely in order to subvert and overthrow that *status quo*. Indeed, it is his use of law that most clearly reveals his ideological roots. In an age dominated by several diverse yet distinct agitations for reform of individual statutes — in England by Bentham's utilitarian legalism, in Ireland by a lawyer-led and at least 25% lawyer-composed[17] Repeal Association — Lalor's appeal to and use of law was certainly not anachronistic. Or so it would seem. However, his basic ideas were firmly rooted in Enlightenment thought and, in particular, in Locke's political and economic notions. He shared with the latter the belief that, as Lichteim could put it, 'Wealth creation was important and beneficial, but the stability of the social system came first.'[18] In addition, his creed 'that every distinct community or nation of men is owner of itself; and can never of right be bound to submit to be governed by another people'[19] is, at root, Locke's principle of government with the consent of the governed. However, whereas Locke used it in order to place a check on the arbitrary use of power by the King, Lalor, following Tom Paine's example,[20] used it to check the arbitrary use of power by both the King and the aristocracy.

In his appeal to popular sovereignty, in his anti-aristocratic sentiments, and in his use of the principle of government by consent of the governed, Lalor is following (consciously or not) in the footsteps of Paine's eighteenth-century 'bourgeois radicalism'.[21] In his appeal to and use of law, he parallels the method, though not the wide-ranging measures, of Bentham's 'philosophical radicalism'.[22] Because law and legal legitimations/rationalisations were at the root of the entrenched aristocratic power which characterised the *ancien régime*, Lalor, like Bentham, attacked those roots in order to discredit and subvert the aristocratic polity. It is in this sense primarily that he was a radical. By going to the legal roots of the system — and radicalism, etymologically, is a derivation from the Latin *radix*, a root[23] — Lalor attacked the foundations on which the traditional social structure was founded.

Eighteenth- and nineteenth-century radicalism was a many-headed hydra, well-nigh impossible to look in the eye and define precisely. There were, for example, agrarian radicals, bourgeois radicals, philosophical radicals, nationalist radicals, democratic radicals; not to mention radical Tories, radical Chartists, radical Liberals, radical Socialists, and so on.[24] The variety was endless. Part of the confusion surrounding the term is, in fact, the result of a quite basic ambiguity. Radical was often used within the confines of existing parties and 'isms' as a synonym for 'extreme'. Hence, for instance, the apparent oxymoron: 'radical Tory'! Essentially, however, and as used here to define Lalor's ideological identity, radical means rational, anti-aristocratic, democratic, reformist (or, when opposition was impervious to reform, revolutionary — in spirit if not in deed). Its foremost spokesmen and propagandists in the late-eighteenth and early-nineteenth centuries, were middle-class men who shared an individualistic, competitive, bourgeois outlook. Given Lalor's position on the rural social ladder in Ireland, one might feasibly contend that he too was a bourgeois radical. His *laissez faire* views of the government's proper economic role, and his respect for the 'English system' of industrialisation (even his moral unease on that subject was matched by almost all radicals of the period) would tend to support such a view. Our intention here, however, is rather more modest; it is merely to remove Lalor from the ideological quicksands of nationalism and socialism. To redefine him as a Radical is to place him more firmly within his age and to rescue him from the clutches of ideological tags which, being retrospectively imposed, all too readily gloss-over or evade the diversity of attitudes, ideas and policies which characterised those involved in Irish politics in the 1840s.

(iii) LALOR'S INFLUENCE

In the wake of the famine and the fiasco of '48, Gavan Duffy's constitutionalism was severely dented but, as Kevin Nowlan correctly remarks, he 'learned one lesson from Fintan Lalor's teachings and [that] was the importance of the agrarian agitation'.[25] Though he retained his preference for parliamentary means of redress, his attitude to tenant politics underwent an enormous change. Previously unwilling (perhaps even unable — by temperament) to look below the middle class for political allies, he had castigated Lalor's ideas on the grounds that: 'His angry peasants, chafing like chained tigers, were creatures of the imagination — not the living people through whom we had to act.'[26] Though there was (and is) considerable bite to this criticism, the real reason for his refusal to involve himself in tenant politics was that 'Lalor's scheme [of a rent strike] would embarrass an unfriendly gentry.'[27]

However, the fundamental underlying flaw in Lalor's plan was less political than social. The famine 'initiated a transformation in the rural social structure'[28] in which holdings of five acres and under fell from 300,000 in 1845 to 88,000 in 1851. Thus, the one-to-ten acre tenants, the constituency which Lalor had attempted to bring within the pale of nationalist and ascendancy politics, were virtually wiped out by the time the Tenant Right League arose in the early 1850s.[29] Granted, Duffy was but a minor deity in that movement (though he would have us believe he was its leading light); nonetheless, that he condescended to become involved at all is due, not only to his conviction that farmers could not agitate successfully without the aid of the urban élite, but also to the constant prodding to which Lalor had subjected him. Not that Fintan would altogether have given his blessing to the Pope's Brass Band. In particular, it fell far short of his own legalistic demands and left the position of the aristocracy fundamentally intact. The 'Three Fs' might ameliorate the tenants' lot; but, for Lalor, such improvements were insignificant and inadequate as long as the aristocratic domination of Irish society remained intact.

Lalor's importance as a theorist, if not an agent, of and for improved conditions for the small-holders has hitherto been overlooked in favour of his alleged influence on the Fenian Brotherhood and later republican nationalists. In fact, despite his acquaintance with John O'Leary and Thomas Clarke Luby, his influence on the fenians was slight. Devoy may well have believed, as Desmond Ryan claims, 'that the roots of Fenianism lay in Lalor [because] he started the small secret society form which Luby and O'Leary built up the Fenian organisation after the crash of '48'.[30] This, however, does not transform the status of his beliefs into facts. Certainly fenianism had its roots in the failures of 1848-9; but, the lessons which it was forced to learn — that an absolutely secret organisation (as opposed to the open 'secret' societies of 1849) was needed if an armed insurrection was to succeed — did not require didactic expositon or explication by Lalor or anyone else. In addition, Lalor's tenant politics — the core of his entire policy and position — were discretely kept at arms length; for, fenianism, like Young Ireland before it, kept its serene distance from anything that smacked even remotely of class conflict. The 'masses', the 'people', the 'nation', were the mysterious constituency of axiomatic patriots which they addressed.

If his influence on the fenians was slight, his influence on the Land War, it might be argued, was surely crucial. Davitt, one of the central agents in that agitation, claimed that as 'the prophet of Irish revolutionary land reform', Lalor had provided the 'seeds . . . for another generation of land reformers'[31] and implies that he personally was the channel through which this was achieved. To assess this claim we need to know not only how and when Davitt came into contact with Lalor's writings/ideas, but also how sure a grasp of those tenets he actually had.

To begin with, we can safely put aside the contention that 'while in prison [he had occupied] himself with reflections on the writings of Fintan Lalor and had come to definite conclusions as to the feasibility, as well as the desirability, of trying Lalor's methods in a modified form';[32] for, the notion that Davitt, a convict on a ticket of leave, emerged from prison with the Land War in his head is patently false. Once free, his first endeavour was to make contact with his fenian brethren — at that time the least likely agents of land agitation. In fact, neither the revolutionaries in the I.R.B. nor the constitutionalists in the Home Rule Party created the Land War, though both proved quite adept at using it in their own interests once it had begun. In the early stages of the struggle Davitt, despite his later claims, advocated policies more in keeping with Duffy's constitutionalism than with Lalor's radicalism. In a lecture in Brooklyn in October 1878, for instance, he advocated a solution to the land question based on co-partnership and argued that Irishmen should seek to penetrate every elective office and support every kind of reform in order to prepare the way for vengeance. At the same meeting, Devoy came out uncompromisingly for the total abolition of landlordism;[33] a fact which validates his later contention that when Davitt visited the United States in 1878 he found the Clan na Gael 'already well versed in the argument (first developed by Fintan Lalor) that the land question could be made the material for victory'.[34] If Devoy and the Clan understood that argument, Davitt certainly did not. For, at Irishtown, when Brennan advocated the sort of 'European' solution favoured by such eminent 'political doctors' as Stein and Hardenberg, Davitt considered him a disciple of Lalor! Continuing to put the shoe on the wrong foot, he described O'Conner Power as 'constitutional and parliamentary' though the latter, at the same meeting, demanded 'the restoration of the land of Ireland to the people of Ireland . . . [by abolishing] landlordism, and making the man who occupies the soil owner of the soil'.[35] Davitt himself only adopted this position in the following August, at the Castlebar convention, when he claimed that 'The land of Ireland belongs to the people of Ireland, to be held and cultivated for the sustenance of those whom god decreed to be inhabitants thereof'. However, the authority he cites for this creed is not Lalor, but 'the English political economist', John Stuart Mill.[36]

Even sharing a platform at Knockaroo in Queen's County with Richard Lalor in 1880 brought him no closer to understanding Fintan's tenets,[37] for Richard's proposals owed little to his deceased brother. As chairman of an earlier meeting in Maryborough (October 1879), Richard had declared that he:

> had not come there to cast odium on the landlords; nor to advise tenants, who were able to pay, not to pay rent. He confined his observations to those who, owing to one of the worst harvests he remembered since the famine, were not in a position to pay their rents. His advice to them was to keep what food would suport them until next September, to keep sufficient seed for the spring crops; and on no account to

part with their stock for the purpose of making up the rent, if doing so would render it impossible for them to provide for their families, and crops for their lands.[38]

Thus, the two most obvious channels by which Davitt could have made an acquaintance with Lalor's ideas (via the Clan na Gael in America, and via Richard Lalor, gentleman farmer and Queen's County M.P.) proved barren. His later copious references to Lalor in his book *The fall of feudalism in Ireland,* are therefore due (and he acknowledges his source) to the publicaiton in 1895 of a small collection of Lalor's writings. The inescapable conclusion, therefore, must be that Davitt used Fintan's ideas to retrospectively legitimise, and provide a 'respectable' intellectual lineage for, his own theories. Moody may be correct in dating Davitt's first full acquaintance with Lalor's writings as late as 1880.[39] However, it should be noted that, even *after* that date, Davitt nowhere indicates that he has a sure grasp of Fintan's major themes: his own land nationalisation policy is, clearly, *not* derived from Lalor's writings; nor is there any evidence that he perceives the legalistic niceties or the physiocratic *laissez-faire* 'developmental' model which underlies Fintan's theories. In addition, whereas the constituency which Lalor had attempted to mobilise in the 1840s consisted primarily of midlands and southern small-holders, those whom Davitt addressed a generation later lived, by and large, on the western coastal fringes. Both in time and in place, therefore, Davitt and Lalor were enormously different from each other.

(iv) CONCLUSIONS

The tenor of Irish political agitation changed enormously in the decade from 1842 to 1852. Repeal and Young Ireland alike had assumed and asserted that political ends would provide the panacea for existing social ills. In aiming for nationalist goals they wooed the landlords and gentry, and argued on the basis of a combination between the middle classes and their social superiors. By the early '50s, such naïvely 'nationalist' political movements had fallen by the wayside, a victim of famine and of their own social romanticism. In the wake of the famine, their place was taken by the Tenant Right League — a narrowly pragmatic movement of and for strong farmers, which (predictably) collapsed when rising prices brought relative prosperity and, its inevitable concommitant, a declining interest in agitation.

Squeezed in between these extremes, there was a brief attempt to mobilise the peasantry for political and social ends. It found its best exponent in Fintan Lalor, though, given the *milieu* in which he came to the fore, the attempt was bound to fail. The peasantry were once more pushed into the wilderness, outside the pale of respectable political action. Whether they ever returned, even during the Land War some thirty years later, is a moot question; that others thought they had does not answer that question. The peasantry whom Davitt had addressed in the 1880s were not those to whom Lalor had looked in 1847. The intervening years had changed them irrevocably. Brought within the ambit of a monetised economy, their aims no less than their means had changed; their structures and their ties to the larger community had changed; prematurely lamented by Davis in 1843, they all but vanished from the rural landscape in the years prior to Independence.

Notes

INTRODUCTION

1 Charles Gavan Duffy, *Four Years of Irish History, 1845-1849,* (London, 1883), p. 464.
2 Duffy, *Four Years of Irish History,* p. 493. (My italics).
3 Duffy, *Four Years of Irish History,* p. 464.
4 Duffy, *Four Years of Irish History,* p. 465. (My italics).
5 Standish O'Grady quoted in T.J. O'Donohue (ed.), *The writings of James Fintan Lalor: with an introduction embodying personal recollections by John O'Leary* (Dublin, 1895), p. xxiv. (My italics). Hereafter referred to as *Lalor*.
6 John Mitchel, *The last conquest of Ireland (perhaps)* (Glasgow, n.d.), p. 195. (My italics).
7 Duffy, *Four Years of Irish History,* p. 473.
8 John O'Leary, *Recollections of fenians and fenianism* (2 vols., London, 1896), i, 35, 29, 38 and 37 respectively.
9 Quoted in Cathal O'Shannon, 'James Fintan Lalor' in M.J. MacManus (ed), *Thomas Davis and Young Ireland* (Dublin, 1945), p. 70. (My italics).
10 O'Donohue, *Lalor*, pp. xxi, xxii, and xxiii respectively.
11 Nathaniel Marlowe (ed), *James Fintan Lalor: collected writings* (Dublin, 1918), pp. vi, viii. He is, no doubt, referring to Fintan's brother, Richard.
12 L. Fogarty, *James Fintan Lalor: patriot and political essayist: 1807-1849* (Dublin, 1918), p. xi. Hereafter abbreviated to *Lalor.*
13 The Socialist Party of Ireland, *The rights of Ireland and the faith of a felon by James Fintan Lalor* (Dublin, n.d.), p. ii.
14 The Socialist Party of Ireland, *The rights of Ireland and the faith of a felon,* p. iii. For the background debate which led up to the publication of the pamphlet (in 1896?) see C. Desmond Greaves, *The life and times of James Connolly* (London, 1976), p. 81; and Samuel Levenson, *A biography of James Connolly* (London, 1977), p. 47.
15 James Connolly, *Labour in Irish History,* (Dublin, 1910); pp. 188-90.
16 P.H. Pearse, *The murder machine and other essays* (Cork, 1976), pp. 83-4, 85.
17 Fogarty, *Lalor,* p. x.
18 Fogarty, *Lalor,* p. xx.
19 Thomas P. O'Neill, 'The papers of James Fintan Lalor in the National Library' in *The Irish Book Lover*, xxx (Jan. 1948), pp. 74-6.
20 Tomás Ó Néill, *Fiontán Ó Leathlobhair* (Dublin, 1962). Hereafter cited as *Ó Leathlobhair*.

21 Joseph Lee, *The modernisation of Irish society: 1848-1918,* (Dublin, 1973), p. 172.

22 Ó Néill, *Ó Leathlobhair,* p. 26. 'Few people, reading this letter for the first time, would fail to be brought to a halt by it. At the same time, no one could say that it was not written in a spirit of sincerity. He was not seeking a bribe . . .'

23 Ó Néill, *Ó Leathlobhair*, p. 27. 'At the time of writing this letter, he was a convinced Conservative, in his heart of hearts'.

CHAPTER 1: LALOR'S LIFE: AN INTERPRETATION

1 Tomas P. O'Neill, 'James Fintan Lalor' in J.W. Boyle (ed.), *Leaders and workers* (Cork, 1978. First edition, 1966), p. 37. Some historians appear to have taken this misleading description at face value without consulting O'Neill's biography. See, for example, Robin Dudley Edwards, *Daniel O'Connell and his world* (London, 1975), p. 89. Robert Kee in *The most distressful country* (vol. 1 of *The green flag*) (London, 1977), p. 259, and George D. Boyce in *Nationalism in Ireland* (Baltimore, Md., 1982), p. 172, both see Pat Lalor as 'a prosperous *Protestant* farmer'. (Emphasis added).

2 Fintan's description of his father's 'class'. See Ó Néill, *Ó Leathlobhair*, p. 25.

3 The farms were located in Tinakill, Tarbert, and Shancartin respectively. Tinakill was originally held on a thirty year lease (see N.L.I., MS 8570) granted in 1767, from John Preston M.P. (later Baron Tara, thanks to the eight votes he put at the disposal of the pro-Union lobby in 1800). The Tarbert farm was first leased to the family in 1791. See Ó Néill, *Ó Leathlobhair*, pp. 2-5.

4 Ó Néill, *Ó Leathlobhair,* p. 14 (My italics). O'Neill is at pains to defend Pat Lalor's record as an improver, though the newspaper report (of 1850) which is his main source is not identified. For an excellent treatment of men of Lalor's class see David Dickson, 'Middlemen' in T. Bartlett and D.W. Hayton (eds.), *Penal era to golden age: essays in Irish history, 1690-1800* (Belfast, 1979), pp. 162-85.

5 James Fintan (1807), Maura (1808), William (1810), Joseph (1812), and Patrick (1814). These were followed by John (1815), Mary (1817), Jerome, Thomas, Catherine, Richard and finally (in 1827) Peter. The names and dates are written on the back of the Tinakill lease (N.L.I., MS 8570). See Ó Néill, *Ó Leathlobhair*, p. 3.

6 *Second report of the Select Committee of the House of Lords appointed to enquire into the collection and payment of tithes in Ireland,* p. 62, H.L. 1831-32 (663), xxii, 242. (Hereafter cited as *Second report . . . Lords*).

7 *Second report . . . Lords,* p. 242.

8 *Second report . . . Lords,* p. 247.

9 See, *Dublin Evening Post* 17, 22 December 1825; Ó Néill, *Ó Leathlobhair*, p. 10.

10 *Leinster Leader,* 31 March 1883; reprinted from *Redpath's Weekly.* See Revd

J. Canon O'Hanlon, Revd E. O'Leary, and Revd M. Lalor, *History of the Queen's County* (2 vols. Dublin, 1907-14), ii, 653 et seq.

11 *Leinster Leader,* 31 March 1883; O'Hanlon, O'Leary, and Lalor, *History of the Queen's County,* ii, 654-5. Ó Néill, *Ó Leathlobhair,* p. 12-14. On the Tithe War see Patrick O'Donohue, 'Causes of the opposition to tithes 1830-8', in *Studia Hibernica* 5 (1965), pp. 7-28; and the same author's 'Opposition to tithe payments in 1830-1', in *Studia Hibernica* 6 (1966), pp. 69-98.

12 *Second report . . . Lords,* p. 242.

13 *Second report . . . Lords,* p. 248.

14 *Second report . . . Lords,* p. 250.

15 *Second report . . . Lords,* p. 250.

16 Oliver MacDonagh, *Ireland: the Union and its aftermath* (London, 1977), p. 15.

17 *Second report . . . Lords,* p. 251.

18 Ó Néill, *Ó Leathlobhair,* pp. 13-14, inexplicably refers only to Lalor's appearance before the Lords' Committee.

19 *Second report from the Select Committee of the House of Commons appointed to enquire into the collection and payment of tithes in Ireland 1831-2,* (508), xxi, questions 3948, 3954 and 3956-8. (Hereafter cited as *Second report . . . Commons*).

20 *Second report . . . Lords,* pp. 252, 256.

21 *Second report . . . Lords,* p. 256.

22 *Second report . . . Lords,* p. 256. Later, (in 1839), Lalor secured the position of Poor Law Guardian for Mountrath and Raheen, and was defeated by only two votes in his bid to become Chairman. See O'Hanlon, O'Leary, and Lalor, *History of the Queen's County,* ii, 693-5.

23 *Second report . . . Lords,* p. 256. I am assuming that, as is his wont, Lalor is using Irish acreage here and have therefore provided equivalent statute acres in parentheses where necessary.

24 *Second report . . . Lords,* pp. 244, and 249 respectively.

25 This is not to deny that Lalor's concerns were justified. The system was clearly unfair to those outside the established church, especially considering that many of those who benefitted from tithes were themselves landowners. For Lalor's 'popular' arguments see *Second report . . . Commons,* Qs 3879, 3880 and 3896.

26 *Second report . . . Commons,* Q 3908. Again, one would need to know Lalor's source here in order to ascertain whether he is using Irish or statute acres. If he is using Irish measure, then the equivalent figure would be an enormous 1,157,870.7 statute acres.

27 *Second report . . . Commons,* Qs 3897, 3898.

28 Indeed, the 'ifs' and 'buts' appended to cover possible shortfalls would tend to suggest that the scheme would not, in practice, be feasible.

29 *Second report . . . Commons,* Q 3928. See also Qs 3917 and 3929. Lalor also argued that tithes should not be appended to current rents (Q 3892), nor be paid to the clergy of *any* denomination (Q 3924).

30 Allegedly O'Connell's description. See O'Hanlon, O'Leary, and Lalor, *History of the Queen's County*, ii, 796. Duffy echoed the sentiment in 1847; see, Fogarty, *Lalor*, p. x. The term was widely used at the time by repealers involved in local politics, to distinguish their candidates from the (by implication) 'dishonest' opposition.

31 B.M. Walker (ed.), *Parliamentary election results in Ireland, 1801-1922* (Dublin, 1978), p. 54. See also Ó Néill, *Ó Leathlobhair*, p. 14.

32 O'Hanlon, O'Leary and Lalor, *History of the Queen's County,* ii, 680 et seq., provides a useful retrospective. For contemporary accounts see *The Leinster Express* for 20 October, and 8, 15, 22, and 29 December 1832. See also Ó Néill's *Ó Leathlobhair*, p. 14.

33 For Maurice Lenihan, later the proprietor of the *Limerick Reporter,* who was charged with putting the new-comer at his ease, the task of befriending Lalor often boiled down to visiting the latter's room and sharing the day's news over a cup of Fintan's undrinkably-strong tea! See Maurice Lenihan, 'Reminiscences of a journalist' in the *Limerick Reporter and Tipperary Vindicator*, 9, 13, 16 Nov. 1866; 26 April, 20 May, 24 Sept., 29 Nov. 1867; 14 Feb. 1868; 20 April 1870. For an account of Lenihan's life and career see F. Finegan's series of articles in *Studies*, vol. xxxv, no. 3 (Sept. 1946), pp. 407-14; vol. xxxvi, nos. 1, 3 (March, Sept. 1947), pp. 97-104 and 358-65; vol. xxxvii, no. 1 (March 1948), pp. 91-6.

34 Lalor is not mentioned on the College's books.

35 Ó Néill, *Ó Leathlobhair*, p. 12.

36 Fogarty, *Lalor,* p. xxi.

37 Fogarty, *Lalor,* p. xxi. In fact no information, 'detailed' or otherwise, exists. The adjective 'detailed' is designed to induce paranoia concerning the possible fate of the alleged 'information'. The same story is repeated, with minor variations, in the 1947 edition, p. xiv.

38 Ó Néill, *Ó Leathlobhair,* p. 12, also believes it unlikely that Lalor was ever in France. See O'Hanlon, O'Leary and Lalor, *History of the Queen's County,* ii, 700. R.F. Foster, however, possibly because he is unacquainted with the secondary literature on Lalor, has revived the chimera of a French connection in *Modern Ireland 1600-1972* (London, 1988), p. 381.

39 Pat Lalor contested the seat in 1835, but ran-in third as a Liberal-Repealer, with 673 votes. Coote headed the poll with 787 votes and the Hon Thomas Vesey was second with 695. Robert Cassidy, Lalor's running mate, brought up the rear with 631 votes. Vesey allegedly threatened to evict his tenants if they failed to support him (Ó Néill, *Ó Leathlobhair*, p. 16). Lalor never ran again, though he did take an active part in local politics. On the 1837 election see O'Hanlon,

O'Leary and Lalor, *History of the Queen's County*, ii, 695 et seq. Coote retained his seat in 1837, 1841, and 1852. He did not run in 1847. See B.M. Walker (ed.), *Parliamentary election results in Ireland*, pp. 59, 65, 71, 78 and 85 respectively.

40 The course was advertised, in these terms, in the *Dublin Evening Post*, 24 July 1817. Reprinted in Revd P. MacSuibhne (ed.), *Knockbeg Centenary Book* (Carlow, 1948), pp. 150-1. Whether Lalor had taken the course or not is not known, though its very existence provides strong circumstantial evidence that it constituted the basis of his later theories.

41 See Ó Néill, *Ó Leathlobhair*, pp. 17-20; and the same author's 'James Fintan Lalor' in J.W. Boyle (ed.), *Leaders and workers*, pp. 37-8. For Conner's career see George O'Brien, 'William Conner' in *Studies*, vol. xii, no. 46 (June 1923), pp. 279-89.

42 Rough draft of aims and affairs of the Society (N.L.I., MS 340). See also Ó Néill, *Ó Leathlobhair*, p. 20; Fogarty, *Lalor*, (1947 ed.), p. xxxvi.

43 *Irish Felon*, 15 July 1848. Reprinted in Fogarty, *Lalor*, (1947 ed.), pp. 105-10. Quotation from p. 105. (All future references will be to this edition, unless otherwise stated). See also *Irish Felon*, 1 July 1848 (Fogarty, *Lalor*, p. 79); reprint of letter dated 25 January 1847 in which Lalor asserts that the Union 'subsisted between Ireland and England for *eighteen* years'. (Emphasis in original).

44 Ó Néill, *Ó Leathlobhair*, p. 22.

45 For the text of the letter, see Ó Néill, *Ó Leathlobhair*, pp. 23-6.

46 Ó Néill, *Ó Leathlobhair*, pp. 130-1. O'Neill, 'James Fintan Lalor' in J.W. Boyle (ed.), *Leaders and workers*, p. 39, is probably over-reacting when he suggests that 'it is possible that the government's decision to follow the banning of the Clontarf repeal meeting and the prosecution of O'Connell with a commission of enquiry into the land question was influenced by Lalor.'

47 Rough draft of article, dated 10 January 1844, in N.L.I., MS 340; partly reprinted in Fogarty, *Lalor*, pp. xvii-xix. This article formed the basis of Lalor's first published letter in *The Nation* in 1847.

48 William emigrated to America in 1837, and Mary married Jerome Fox soon after; see Ó Néill, *Ó Leathlobhair*, pp. 15, 33.

49 Jerome to Fintan, 13 February 1845; Mary Fox (Lalor) to Fintan, 2 and 20 July 1845; William Blood to Fintan, 7 July 1845 (N.L.I., MS 340). Fintan to Richard, 12 April; 19, 25 June 1845 (N.L.I., MS 8563). Ó Néill, *Ó Leathlobhair*, p. 33.

50 Testimonies from Cane, 6 October 1845; Thomas Brady, Prof. of Jurisprudence, Royal College of Physicians, 7 October 1845; and Archibald Fitzpatrick, M.R.C.S.I., 6 October 1845 (N.L.I., MS 340). Fintan to his father, 7 August, 23 October, 12 November 1845 (N.L.I., MS8563).

51 See Ó Néill, *Ó Leathlobhair*, pp. 35-7, and 51 et seq.

52 O'Neill, 'James Fintan Lalor' in Boyle (ed.), *Leaders and workers*, p. 39, sees the famine as being 'crucial' for Lalor's reëmergence.

53 Duffy, *Four Years of Irish History*, p. 470. According to Fogarty, *Lalor*, (1918 ed.), p. xxv: 'Most of his letters were circulated among the Confederates, *four* only being published in the *Nation*.' (My italics). In fact, only *three* were published. See Ó Néill, *Ó Leathlobhair*, pp. 54-5.

54 Duffy, *Four Years of Irish History*, p. 470.

55 Duffy to Lalor, no date (N.L.I., MS340). Fintan and his brother Richard joined the Irish Confederation in April 1847. See Ó Néill, *Ó Leathlobhair*, p. 52.

56 Ó Néill, *Ó Leathlobhair*, p. 58. Duffy, *Four Years of Irish History*, p. 477 and 484 et seq. The committee comprised Dillon, Smith O'Brien and Devin Reilly.

57 Both quotations from Duffy, *Four Years of Irish History*, p. 486.

58 Duffy, *Four Years of Irish History*, p. 489.

59 Duffy, *Four Years of Irish History*, p. 487. In a letter to the Confederation dated January 25, 1847 (see draft N.L.I., MS 340), Lalor spoke of 'taking quiet and peaceable possession of all the rights, and powers of government, and proceeding quietly to exercise them'. This is Duffy's policy without the dramatic prose ('seizing' positions of power, etc). Lalor's letter, with minor emendations, was published in the *Felon*, 1 July 1848; reprinted in Fogarty, *Lalor*, pp. 67-83.

60 Trenwith to Fintan, 21 April, 7 May, and Sept. 1847 (N.L.I., MS 340). Ó Néill, *Ó Leathlobhair*, pp. 61 et seq.

61 Duffy gives a gleeful resumé in *Four Years of Irish History*, pp. 493 et seq. Fogarty, in the 'Introduction' to the 1918 edition of *Lalor*, (pp. xxv-xxvi), waxes self-righteously indignant on Lalor's behalf, casting dark aspersions on the un-patriotic Mr Conner, 'the Farmers' Friend': 'Why this uninvited speaker should have intruded to thwart the scheme of Lalor and Doheny, remains unexplained. It would be interesting to find if he actually undertook the journey from Dublin to Holycross out of pure "friendship" for the farmers.' Ó Néill, *Ó Leathlobhair*, pp. 61-73, wonderfully reconstructs the embarrassing débâcle, but is slow to interpret its significance. See the *Freeman's Journal*, 20 Sept. 1847. The *Nation's* report is reprinted in Fogarty, *Lalor*, (both editions), pp. 47 et seq.

62 Mitchel to Lalor, 4 Jan. 1848; reprinted in Fogarty, *Lalor*, pp. 120-3. Quotations from p. 122.

63 *Irish Felon*, 24 June 1848; reprinted in Fogarty, *Lalor*, pp. 52-66. Quotation from p. 52.

64 *Irish Felon*, 1 July 1848, contains the entire text of Lalor's original letter to the Confederation, complete with introductory remarks referring to Mitchel's reply. Reprinted in Fogarty, *Lalor*, pp. 67-83.

65 Mitchel to Smith O'Brien, 8 August 1847, and 8 Sept. 1847; reprinted in part in Fogarty, *Lalor*, pp. 125-7. Compare these remarks with Mitchel's later confession to Lalor (4 Jan. 1848): 'I am ashamed . . . to admit, that on *the only question we ever differed about* I was wholly wrong. Last summer the time had come

for giving up the humbug of "conciliating classes" winning landlords over to nationality and the rest of it.' Reprinted in Fogarty, op. cit., pp. 120-3. (Italics added).

Mitchel, though he was always more than a mere disciple, clearly owed a great deal to Lalor. Compare, for instance, his prospectus for the *United Irishman* — reprinted in P.S. O'Hegary's *John Mitchel: an appreciation, with some account of Young Ireland* (Dublin, 1917), pp. 68-9 — with any of Lalor's letters to either *The Nation* or the *Felon*.

66 Fogarty, *Lalor,* p. 91. See also Rachel O'Higgins, 'The Irish influence in the Chartist movement' in *Past and Present,* no. 20 (November 1961), pp. 83-96.

67 Mitchel's description as quoted by E.R.R. Green in, 'The beginnings of fenianism' in T.W. Moody (ed.), *The fenian movement* (Cork, 1978), p. 12.

68 See O'Neill's, 'James Fintan Lalor' in Boyle (ed.), *Leaders and workers*, p. 42.

69 David Thomson's description in *England in the nineteenth century* (Harmondsworth, 1950), p. 5.

70 See Gearóid Ó Tuathaigh, *Ireland before the famine: 1798-1848* (Dublin, 1972), p. 200.

71 See Joy MacAskill's 'The Chartist land plan' in Asa Briggs (ed.), *Chartist studies* (London, 1959), p. 304-41.

72 According to Gavan Duffy — *The league of north and south: an episode in Irish history, 1850-4* (London, 1886), pp. 394-5 — Mitchel was 'an habitual reader of the *Northern Star* in '48; every number of [his] paper contained extracts from it. [He] was in personal communication with the Irish Chartists, and spoke at two of the three meetings they held in Dublin in that year. In the *Star,* Mr Feargus O'Connor published a biography [of him].' So there can be no doubting his 'growing Chartist popularity' prior to his demise.

73 Duffy, *The league of north and south,* p. 392.

74 See Ó Néill, *Ó Leathlobhair*, pp. 88-9.

75 Duffy, *Four Years of Irish History,* p. 543.

76 Fogarty, *Lalor*, pp. xxxvi-xxxvii; see also pp. xxiv and 154-5 for details of the proposed journal, *The Newgate Calendar.*

77 C.G. Duffy, *My life in two hemispheres* (London, 1888), p. 315.

78 O'Neill, 'James Fintan Lalor' in Boyle (ed.), *Leaders and workers,* p. 43. See also O'Neill's 'Fintan Lalor and the 1849 movement' in *An Cosantóir: the Irish defence journal,* x, no. 4(April, 1950), pp. 173-9.

79 O'Neill, 'James Fintan Lalor' in Boyle (ed.), *Leaders and workers,* p. 44.

80 John O'Leary, *Recollections,* i, 39-41.

81 Duffy, *Four Years of Irish History*, p. 473.

82 O'Leary, *Recollections,* i, 37.

83 Quoted by Cathal O'Shannon, 'James Fintan Lalor' in MacManus (ed.), *Thomas Davis and Young Ireland,* pp. 69-70. (My italics).

84 Duffy, *Four Years of Irish History*, p. 465.

85 Fogarty, *Lalor,* (1918 ed.), pp. xxvii and xxvi. (My italics).
86 Ó Néill, *Ó Leathlobhair*, pp. 25-6. (Italics in original).
87 Fogarty, *Lalor*, p. 1.
88 See Robert Kee, *The most distressful country*, pp. 235-6 for 'Young', 'Old' and 'Middle-aged' Ireland; p. 262 for 'Infant' Ireland.
89 Ó Néill, *Ó Leathlobhair*, p. 26. (Italics in original).
90 A comparison of Lalor's contributions to both the *Nation* and the *Felon*, together with his surviving private correspondence, indicates that his basic principles remained relatively constant throughout the 1840s. Many of his later published letters were in fact based almost verbatim on earlier private essays and letters; for example, the article which led to the break with his father (rough draft, dated 10 January 1844, in N.L.I., MS 340; partly reprinted in Fogarty, *Lalor,* pp. xviii-xix) later formed the basis of his first published letter in the *Nation* in 1847.

CHAPTER 2: LALOR'S APPEAL TO LAW

1 E.L. Woodward, *The age of reform (1815-70)* (rev. ed.; London, 1962).
2 Edward Royle, *Radical politics 1790-1900: religion and unbelief* (London, 1971), p. 101. (My italics).
3 William Blackstone, *Commentaries on the laws of England* 4 vols. (15th ed.; London, 1809). Hereafter referred to as *Commentaries.*
4 Blackstone, *Commentaries,* i, 6. As Strauss and Cropsey remark: 'Dizzy with the effort to comprehend the reason of a system where, for example, a brother of the half blood may never succeed as heir to the estate of his elder brother even if they have the same father, the reader is likely to conclude that the old maxim of the common lawyer that 'what is not reason is not law' is maintained only by an unshakable determination to assert, however artifically and at whatever cost in Latin maxims and in patchwork fictions, that what is English law is reason.' Leo Strauss and Joseph Cropsey (eds.), *History of political philosophy,* (Chicago, 1963), p. 544.
5 Blackstone, *Commentaries,* iv, 443. (Emphasis in original).
6 A.V. Dicey, *Law and opinion in England during the nineteenth century* (London, 1905), p. 72. See also F.W. Maitland and F.C. Montague, *A sketch of English legal history* (New York, 1951), pp. 161-89; Carl Joachim Friedrich, *The philosophy of law in historical perspective* (2nd ed.; Chicago, London, 1963), p. 242 believes that 'the isolation of English law and the conceit common to the guild that English law is something unique' has been a major obstacle to legal history. 'History', he wrote, quoting Maitland, 'involves comparison and the English lawyer who knew nothing and cared nothing for any system but his own hardly came in sight of legal history. . . . An isolated system cannot explain itself, still less explain its history.' Hence, the myopic, self-assured, aura of superiority which Blackstone and others exhude. See also Robert Blake's *The*

Conservative Party from Peel to Churchill (London, 1979), pp. 12-14, for an excellent debunking of such attitudes.

7 Dicey, *Law and opinion in England,* p. 63.

8 As MacDonagh, *Ireland,* p. 17, aptly quips: ' "forever" was a sort of incantation in the Act'.

9 MacDonagh, *Ireland,* p. 9.

10 MacDonagh, *Ireland,* p. 13.

11 See Angus MacIntyre, *The Liberator,* (London, 1965), pp. 302-8. This underlying legalist bias was just as evident among the Young Irelanders, (e.g., Davis, Mitchel, D'Arcy McGee, etc.).

12 Fogarty, *Lalor*, p. 1.

13 Fogarty, *Lalor*, p. 62.

14 Fogarty, *Lalor*, p. 4.

15 Ó Néill, *Ó Leathlobhair,* p. 141, uses the 16th edition of Blackstone's *Commentaries* (London, 1826) edited by Joseph Chitty, in which the spelling is modernised. I have used the 15th edition (London, 1809) as internal evidence, specifically the footnotes provided by Edward Christianson, suggests that this was the edition used by Lalor.

16 The starting point is conventional enough, especially the reliance on natural law. Blackstone uses the same format in the *Commentaries* i, 1 et seq. But as J. Walter Jones aptly remarks: 'natural law was identical in Blackstone's eyes with the law of England'. *Historical introduction to the theory of law* (Oxford, 1940), p. 90.

17 For an excellent discussion of this see, W. Friedmann, *Legal theory* (2nd ed.; London, 1949), Chapters 3, 7, 8 and 9; pp. 15-17, 35-57.

18 Fogarty, *Lalor*, p. 99. However, Lalor's claim to have been starved of knowledge should be taken with a pinch of salt. John O'Leary states that 'Of books, by the way, we talked much; indeed I think most of our talk was of books, though of necessity much of it was political, and some of it politico-economical, owing to Lalor's peculiar theories on the land question'.

19 Fogarty, *Lalor*, p. 100.

20 *Commentaries,* ii, 7. (My italics).

21 Fogarty, *Lalor*, p. 101.

22 Lalor to Mitchel, June 1847; reprinted in Fogarty, *Lalor,* p. 44.

23 Fogarty, *Lalor*, pp. 97 and 99. (Emphasis in original).

24 Quotations from Fogarty, *Lalor*, pp. 10 and 61 respectively.

25 Fogarty, *Lalor*, pp. 10, 13-14.

26 Fogarty, *Lalor*, pp. 10-11.

27 Fogarty, *Lalor*, pp. 13 and 19 respectively. Nor was Lalor alone in this conviction. J.V. Stewart in *A letter to Lord Clarendon* (Letterkenny, 1849), similarly argued that 'The famine caused the permanent uprooting of the whole social system'.

28 Fogarty, *Lalor*, p. 13. (Italics in original).
29 Fogarty, *Lalor*, p. 13.
30 Fogarty, *Lalor*, pp. 17-18.
31 Fogarty, *Lalor*, pp. 13, 17 and 43.
32 Fogarty, *Lalor*, p. 63.
33 Fogarty, *Lalor*, p. 80.
34 Fogarty, *Lalor*, pp. 76-7. As no such law exists for Ireland, Lalor opted for a rent-strike to achieve the same ends.
35 Fogarty, *Lalor*, pp. 74-5. Based on the principle of government with the consent of the governed.
36 Fogarty, *Lalor*, p. 57; see also p. 60.
37 *Commentaries,* ii, 18. (Italics in original). The maxim should actually read: '*Cujus est, solum ejus est usque ad coelum et ad inferos*'. (Whose is the soil, his is also that which is up to the sky and down to the depths of the earth.') This is almost verbatim, Lalor's basic tenet 'that the entire ownership of Ireland, moral and material, up to the sun, and down to the centre, is vested of right in the people of Ireland' (Fogarty, *Lalor*, p. 60). For a basic but extremely useful introduction to the topic see L.B. Curzon, *Land Law* (2nd ed.; London, 1975), which also contains a useful bibliography.
38 Fogarty, *Lalor*, pp. 16, 17.
39 Lord Croke, as quoted by L.B. Curzon, *Land Law,* p. 8. See also, *Commentaries,* ii, 50, 53, and 59.
40 *Commentaries,* i, 247; ii, 259; and, Fogarty, *Lalor,* p. 104.
41 Fogarty, *Lalor*, p. 102; see also, pp. 49 and 95.
42 Foster, *Modern Ireland,* p. 314n is the most notable recent example of this common misinterpretation. Raymond D. Crotty, *Irish agricultural production: its volume and structure* (Cork, 1966), pp. 63-4, lays rather more stress than most on the assumed role of the State in Lalor's scheme. As Lalor's distrust of orthodox political institutions was so entrenched (see below, Chapter 5), it is by no means clear what role he envisaged for the State. At any rate, in asserting that Lalor's theories were 'a reversal to the principles upheld by the Brehon law', Crotty is erroneously implying Irish roots for Lalor's (adapted English) legalism.
43 Quotations from Fogarty, *Lalor,* pp. 68, 66, 37, 62, 44, 64 and 44 respectively.
44 Lalor couches the whole issue of 'new titles' and 'old' in legal parlance. There is little evidence, however, that he thought the aristocracy likely to declare its willingness to 'hold in fee from the Irish nation'. See Fogarty, *Lalor,* pp. 64, 95, and 130. See also *The Nation's* account of the Holycross resolutions, especially number six; reprinted in Fogarty, *Lalor,* pp. 47 et seq; and the rough draft of Fintan's speech for the occasion, in N.L.I., MS 340.
45 Fogarty, *Lalor,* p. 43.
46 An indication of the volume of pamphlets on the topic can be readily gleaned

from R.D. Collison Black's *A catalogue of pamphlets on economic subjects (1750-1900) in Irish libraries* (Belfast, 1969); pp. 287-367 cover the decade 1840-9 inclusive. The same author's *Economic thought and the Irish question, 1817-70* (Cambridge, 1960), is an excellent guide through the bewildering jungle of conflicting opinions and theories.

47 *Report from H.M. Commissioners of inquiry into the state of the law and practice in respect to the occupation of land in Ireland* H.C. 1845, (605), (606), xix; (616), xx; (657), xxi; (672) (673), xxii. Hereafter cited as *Devon Commission.*

48 *Reports of the Parliamentary Committee of the Loyal National Repeal Association* (3 vols.; Dublin, 1844-46); 'First report on the land question', ii, 295-9, with appendix (pp. i-c); 'Second report on the land question', ii, 317-8; 'Third report on the land question', ii, 319-36. Hereafter cited as *Repeal Reports.*

49 See 'Second report on the land question' in *Repeal Reports,* ii, 317. Absenteeism and the drain of specie are treated in Ch. 3 of Black's *Economic thought and the Irish quesiton,* pp. 72-85. See also G.L. Barrow, *The emergence of the Irish banking system, 1820-45* (Dublin, 1975), pp. 56, 191; and the same author's 'The use of money in mid-nineteenth century Ireland', *Studies,* lix, no. 233 (Spring, 1970), pp. 81-8. Joseph Lee's 'The dual economy in Ireland 1800-50' in T.D. Williams (ed.), *Historical Studies,* viii (Dublin, 1971), is a valuable contribution to a complex problem.

50 'Third report on the land question' in *Repeal Reports,* ii, 324; see recommendations 22, 26 and 27.

51 *Repeal Reports,* ii, 321, 323; recommendations 2 and 15. (My italics).

52 'Third report on the land question', *Repeal Reports,* ii, 326-7. (My italics).

53 See 'Third general report', *Repeal reports,* iii, 119-60; especially p. 153 on 'the general objects we have had in view in framing these Reports'.

54 'Third report on the land question' in *Repeal Reports,* ii, 320; and ii, 148, 153 respectively.

55 See, 'A year's work', reprinted in *The voice of the Nation: a manual of nationality* (Dublin, 1844), pp. 187-93. Quotations from p. 192. (Italics in original).

56 See 'Landlordism in Ulster', and 'The rights and wrongs of property' in *The voice of the Nation,* pp. 143-9 and 65-7; quotations from pp. 148 and 67 respectively.

57 See 'Crime in Tipperary' in *The voice of the Nation,* pp. 22-4; quotation pp. 23,24. (Italics in original).

58 See 'Aristocratic institutions', *The voice of the Nation,* pp. 90-5; quotation from p. 91.

59 See Duffy's 'The right of the landlord' in *The voice of the Nation,* pp. 173-6; quotations from pp. 175 and 176.

60 See 'A year's work' in *The voice of the Nation,* pp. 187-93; quotation from pp. 187-8. (Italics in original).

61 For Crawford's views, in the context of their times, see Black, *Economic thought and the Irish question,* pp. 27-9, 36-8, 43-6, 62, 101 and 225.

62 *Hansard,* 3rd series, vol. lxxi, column 419 (19 August 1843).

63 Conner was quite probably the most prolific pamphleteer in Ireland; he was certainly the most dogged! He was the author of *The speech of William Conner Esq., against rackrents, etc.* (Dublin, 1832); *The true political economy of Ireland; or rackrent the one great cause of all her evils, with its remedy* (Dublin, 1835); *The axe laid to the root of Irish oppression* (Dublin, 1840); *The prosecuted speech delivered in proposing a petition to Parliament in favour of a valuation and a perpetuity of his farm to the tenant, etc.* (Dublin, 1842); *A letter to the tenantry of Ireland containing an exposition of the rackrent system* (Dublin, 1850); and *The catechism of valuation and perpetuity of tenure* (3rd ed.; Dublin, 1850). See also Black, *Economic thought and the Irish question,* pp. 24-9.

64 *The speech . . . against rackrents,* p. 5.

65 *The speech . . . against rackrents,* p. 23.

66 *Commentaries,* i, 268. Blackstone would have been horrified not only by the recklessness with which Lalor redecorated the 'ancient pile' to suit Irish conditions, but also by the irresponsible manner in which he ripped it from its foundations in English custom and transplanted it whole and entire to Ireland.

67 Strauss and Cropsey (eds.), *History of political philosophy,* provides an excellent debunking of Blackstone's approach to law; quotation from p. 545.

68 Both these terms are from Lawrence C. Becker's brilliantly lucid study *Property rights: philosophic foundations* (London, 1977), p. 2.

69 *Irish Felon,* 24 June 1848; rough draft in N.L.I., MS 340; reprinted in Fogarty, *Lalor,* p. 64. (Italics in original).

70 Lalor to Mitchel; reprinted in Fogarty, *Lalor,* pp. 42-6. Quotations from p. 44. (Italics in original).

71 *Irish Felon,* 8 July 1848; 'The faith of a felon', reprinted in Fogarty, *Lalor,* pp. 92-105. Quotation from p. 98. (My italics).

72 *Irish Felon,* 8 July 1848; reprinted in Fogarty, *Lalor,* p. 94. (Italics in original).

73 *Irish Felon,* 8 July 1848; reprinted in Fogarty, *Lalor,* p. 96; *Nation,* 24 April 1847. Rough draft in N.L.I., MS 340; reprinted in Fogarty, *Lalor,* p. 14.

CHAPTER 3: LALOR'S USE OF 'CLASS'

1 Burke did, in fact, use the term 'class'. See *Reflections on the Revolution in France* edited and with an introduction by Conor Cruise O'Brien (Harmondsworth, 1969); for example, pp. 135, 228 and 243. (Hereafter cited as *Reflections*). 'Rank', 'order', and 'estate' are, however, the essence of his vocabulary, and 'class' when used is either a very general term or a synonym for 'rank'.

2 The appeal to law as a fundamental corner-stone of the old order is evident in

almost every page of the *Reflections*. See, for example, pp. 96-100, 106, 108-11, 113, 115-9, and 193. According to one authority on the period, 'French society of the ancien régime was defined mainly in juridic terms'. See J.Q.C. Mackrell's scholarly and informative study, *The attack on 'Feudalism' in eighteenth-century France* (London, 1973), p. 51.

3 Raymond Williams, *Culture and society, 1780-1950* (Harmondsworth, 1963), p. 15.

4 See Asa Briggs, 'The language of "class" in early nineteenth-century England' in A. Briggs and J. Saville (eds.), *Essays in labour history* (London, 1967), p. 47. The first monograph on this topic was A.E. Bestor's excellent 'The evolution of the Socialist vocabulary' in the *Journal of the History of Ideas,* vol. ix, no. 3 (June 1948), pp. 259-302. See also, R.S. Neale, 'Class and class consciousness in early nineteenth century England: three classes or five?', *Victorian Studies,* xii (1968), pp. 4-32.

5 Lord Brougham, quoted in Raymond Williams, *Keywords: a vocabulary of culture and society* (Glasgow, 1976), p. 53; on the emergence of the middle class see pp. 53, 54, 55. See also, A. Briggs, 'The language of "class" in early nineteenth-century England' in Briggs and Saville (eds.), *Essays in labour history,* pp. 52-9.

Compare Brougham's quasi-economic 'definition' of 'the people' here, with Burke's juridic approach of the previous century: 'In a state of *rude* nature', Burke claimed, 'there is no such thing as a people. A number of men in themselves have no collective capacity. The idea of a people is the idea of a corporation. It is wholly artificial; and made, like all legal fictions by common agreement.' Burke, 'Appeal from the New to the Old Whigs' (1791) in E.J. Payne (ed.), *Burke: select works* (Oxford, 1878), iii, 82. (Emphasis in original).

6 Patricia Hollis (ed.), *Class and class conflict in nineteenth-century England 1815-50* (London, 1973), p. xxi.

7 See Stephen Coltham's 'The Bee-Hive newspaper: its origins and early struggles' in Briggs and Saville (eds.), *Essays in labour history,* pp. 174-204.

8 See Williams, *Keywords,* p. 54. 'Indolence' and 'industry' represented, at root, the same bi-polar dichotomy as 'Aristocracy' and 'the People'.

9 The notion that class is *horizontal,* whilst other forms of stratification are vertical, is a vulgar error perpetrated by sociologists. It has been perpetuated, unfortunately, by those historians who lament the (alleged) passing of the old order. F.M.L. Thompson, for example, defends the old vocabulary of sectoral 'interests' as a truer reflection of 'a society in which vertical divisions by sources of livelihood seemed . . . more real and important than horizontal divisions by class'. *English landed society in the nineteenth century* (London, 1963), p. 5. Thompson's humorous opening paragraph, in which the changed fortunes of aristocrats are likened to those of the horse ('dignified and recreational rather than functional'), is his most perceptive insight in an otherwise disappointing

book. For a wittier and more perceptive critique, see Michael Young's brilliant little essay *The rise of the meritocracy* (Harmondsworth, 1961). 'In our island', he writes (p. 48), 'we never discarded the values of the aristocracy, because we never discarded the aristocracy. It displayed an amazing resilience which allowed it, as so often in previous centuries, to disappoint the many critics waiting to attend its funeral.'

10 The most obvious examples were the voluminous *Reports of the commission for inquiring into the condition of the poorer classes in Ireland* H.C., 1835 (309) xxxii; 1836 (35), (43) xxx; 1836 (36) xxxi; 1836 (37) xxxii; 1836 (38) xxxiii; 1836 (39) (40) (41) xxxiv; 1837 (68) xxxi, all of which use 'class' terminology in a broad, descriptive sense. The earliest 'official' examples I came across were in the *Minutes of evidence taken before the select committee of the House of Lords, appointed to examine into the nature and extent of the disturbances which have prevailed in those districts of Ireland which are now subject to the provisions of the Insurrection Act* H.L., 1825 (200), vii. See also, Pat Lalor's evidence in the *Second report of the . . . House of Commons on tithes,* (in 1832) question 3905; and his evidence before the *Devon Commission,* (in 1845), pp. 326 et seq.

11 See Joy MacAskill's 'The Chartist land plan' in Briggs (ed.), *Chartist studies,* pp. 304-41. See also J.T. Ward's *Chartism* (London, 1973), and F.C. Mather's *Chartism* (London, 1977), for a fuller account not only of the movement but of the considerable overlap of ideas and issues between Chartists and Repealers. Rachel O'Higgins, 'The Irish influence in the Chartist movement' in *Past and Present,* no. 20 (Nov., 1961), pp. 83-96, is useful but dated.

12 An indication of the emergence and use of general class terms (e.g., 'poorer classes', 'industrious classes', 'useful classes') can be readily gleaned from a perusal of the titles listed in Black's *A catalogue of pamphlets on economic subjects.*

13 Examples could be multiplied *ad infinitum.* The earliest I have come across is in the *Freeman's Journal,* 16 July 1811, where 'the lower classes of the Protestant inhabitants of Mountrath' (Queen's Co./Laois) are taken to task for their 'disgraceful and outrageous' conduct during the local July 12 (Orange) celebrations.

14 Here again, examples (especially in the 1830s and afterwards) are voluminous. The earliest use of 'class' which I have come across in an Irish magazine is in an article on 'Sinecures and taxes' in the *Dublin Examiner or Monthly miscellany of science, literature and art,* vol. i, no. vi (Oct. 1816), p. 454; see also 'Plan for payment of the national debt' in ibid., vol. ii, no. viii (Dec. 1816), p. 146. Essentially the same general, descriptive usage is to be found in later periodicals; see, for example, *The Irish monthly magazine of politics and literature* vol. i, no. v (Sept. 1832), p. 340 (article on 'Parliamentary pledges').

15 Marx to Engels, 4 Dec. 1869; reprinted in *Marx/Engels: Ireland and the Irish*

question (Moscow, London, 1978), pp. 395-6. (Italics in original).

16 Engels to Marx, 9 Dec. 1869, in *Marx/Engels,* pp. 396-7.

17 See Nicholas Mansergh, *The Irish question 1840-1921* (3rd ed.; London, 1975), pp. 103-31 ('The Communist International and the Irish question').

18 *Devon Commission,* question 29.

19 *Devon Commission,* Q. 63.

20 *Devon Commission,* Q. 32.

21 *Devon Commission,* Q. 29. Such disingenuous advice is disarming! No doubt the cost of reducing the social distance between landlord and tenant accounted for the 'higher rent'!

22 *Devon Commission,* Q. 51. For Lalor, who was deeply involved in local politics, this was a prime consideration. He had fallen victim to landlord politics in 1835 when Sir Charles Coote, the largest landholder in the county, and Hon Thomas Vesey, played the 'peasant thrump' and ousted him as M.P. for County Laois.

23 *Devon Commission,* Q. 55.

24 *Devon Commission,* Q. 52.

25 T.W. Rolleston (ed.), *Prose writings of Thomas Davis* (London, n.d.) pp. 2, 7. Hereafter referred to as *Davis.*

26 Rolleston (ed.), *Davis,* p. 7.

27 Rolleston (ed.), *Davis,* p. 24. Whether a product of paranoia or of blinkered provincialism, 'the stranger' is a frequent, if enigmatic, 'traveller' on the fringes of Davis' prose. As a concept it deserves rather more attention and analysis than I have been able to give it here.

28 Rolleston (ed.), *Davis,* pp. 174 et seq.

29 Kee, *The most distressful country,* p. 195. See also MacDonagh, *Ireland,* p. 152, on Davis' flirtation with English radical politics prior to his involvement in either *The Nation* or Repeal.

30 Kee, *The most distressful country,* p. 196.

31 Duffy, *Four years of Irish History,* p. 483.

32 Rolleston (ed.), *Davis,* p. 25.

33 Rolleston (ed.), *Davis,* pp. 174-6.

34 Rolleston (ed.), *Davis,* pp. 177.

35 Rolleston (ed.), *Davis,* pp. 177.

36 Rolleston (ed.), *Davis,* pp. 177-8.

37 Rolleston (ed.), *Davis,* p. 24.

38 Rolleston (ed.), *Davis,* pp. 40 and 11 respectively.

39 See, 'The rights and wrongs of property' in *Voice of the Nation,* p. 67. (Italics in original).

40 Duffy, *Four years of Irish History,* p. 483.

41 Arthur Griffith (ed.), *Meagher of the sword. Speeches of Thomas Francis Meagher in Ireland 1846-8* (Dublin, 1917), p. 89.

42 Griffith (ed.), *Meagher of the sword,* p. 81; see also, pp. 100 and 225.

43 L. Fogarty, *Father John Kenyon, a patriot priest of forty-eight* (Dublin, n.d.), pp. 88 and 93-4 respectively.

44 Lalor to Mitchel, 21 June 1847; reprinted in Fogarty, *Lalor*, p. 43.

45 Fogarty, *Lalor*, p. 20.

46 These points, taken together, should provide ample proof that class (either as concept or relationship) is not a pure entity. As E.P. Thompson explains — *The making of the English working class* (Harmondsworth, 1968), p. 9 — no sociological net, no matter how finely meshed, can hope to discover or portray a 'pure' specimen of class or class strata. Nor is the reason far to find, though it is not the one Thompson invokes: Class, like Beauty, exists in the eye of the beholder! (This, however, does not necessarily imply that it is only skin deep!)

Thompson (p. 11) rightly takes Ralph Darendorf to task for an 'obsessive' concern with 'methodology', and castigates him for failing to examine 'a single real class situation in a real historical situation'. Yet, Thompson's ideas on class, despite their historically specific contextualisation, are at least as problematic as Dahrendorf's ahistorical abstractions. For instance, to assert (pp. 9-10) that 'class happens when some men, as a result of common experiences (inherited or shared), feel and articulate the identity of their interests as between themselves, and as against other men whose interests are different from (and largely opposed to) theirs', is to solve nothing. Under the (sexist?) terms of this criterion, 'nationalism' and 'class' are similar, if not in fact identical, phenomena. A 'definition' which is broad (or loose?) enough to encompass the making of *both* 'the English working class' and of Irish nationalism is, patently, defunct.

However, given Thompson's xenophobic treatment of the rôle of the Irish in the making of the 'English' working class, the rich irony of this unexpected outcome affords a certain perverse satisfaction!

47 Fogarty, *Lalor*, pp. 13-14.

48 Fogarty, *Lalor*, p. 7.

49 Fogarty, *Lalor*, p. 7.

50 Both quotations from Fogarty, *Lalor,* p. 60.

51 Fogarty, *Lalor*, p. 22.

52 See Lalor's letter to Peel, quoted in full in Tomás Ó Néill's *Ó Leathlobhair,* p. 26.

53 Fogarty, *Lalor*, pp. 62-3.

54 The total number of 'landed proprietors' was first estimated in 1861 at 8,412 persons. Black (*Economic thought and the Irish question,* p. 5) believes 'a reasonable estimate for the pre-famine period would be about 10,000 landowners in a population of 8,000,000.'

55 Fogarty, *Lalor*, p. 28.

56 *Returns of agricultural produce in Ireland in the year 1847: — Part 1. Tillage*

returns, H.C. 1847-8 (923), lvii, p. 15.

57 *Devon Commission,* Appendix 95, (i), p. 288, H.C. 1845 (672), xxiii.

58 Fogarty, *Lalor*, p. 28.

59 Fogarty, *Lalor*, pp. 28 and 30.

60 Fogarty, *Lalor*, p. 27.

61 *Report of the commissioners appointed to take the census of Ireland for the year 1841* H.C. 1843 (504), xxiv, pp. 434-5.

62 *Census of Ireland . . . 1841,* pp. xxiii.

63 Fogarty, *Lalor*, pp. 26-7; catalogue of books at Tinakill, 20 March 1860 (N.L.I., MS 8570). Ó Néill, *Ó Leathlobhair,* p. 39.

64 Fogarty, *Lalor*, p. 35. (My italics).

65 See Fogarty, *Lalor*, pp. 26-37. The 231,000 families of p. 27, become 230,000 on p. 35; and, the 510,000 families of p. 28 are inexplicably reduced to 500,000 on pp. 31 and 35 respectively.

66 Fogarty, *Lalor*, p. 68.

67 Fogarty, *Lalor*, p. 110.

68 Quotations from Fogarty, *Lalor*, pp. 111, and 86, 87 respectively. (Italics in original).

CHAPTER 4: LALOR'S ECONOMIC 'THEORIES'

1 Donald Winch, 'The emergence of economics as a science 1750-1870', in Carlo M. Cipolla (ed.), *The Fontana economic history of Europe,* (6 vols.; Glasgow, 1972-6), iii, 514.

2 David Ricardo, *Principles of political economy and taxation* (London, 1817); Revd T. Malthus, *Principles of political economy, considered with a view to their practical application* (London, 1820); J.R. McCulloch, *Principles of political economy: with a sketch of the rise and progress of the science* (2nd ed.; London, 1830), and the same author's *The literature of political economy* (London, 1845); J.S. Mill, *Principles of political economy, with some of their applications to social philosophy* (London, 1848).

3 Adam Smith, quoted by Donald Winch, 'The emergence of economics as a science' in Cipolla (ed.), *Economic history of Europe,* iii, 515.

4 John Locke, *Two treatises of government,* (with an introduction and notes by Peter Laslett), (New York, 1965). See *The second treatise of government,* Ch. V, propositions 27, 28, pp. 328-30.

5 For an excellent treatment of this topic from an unusual perspective see Paul J. McNulty, *The origins and development of labor economics* (Cambridge, Mass., 1980), especially Chs. 2 and 3, pp. 38-90. See also Thomas Sowell, *Classical economics reconsidered* (Princeton, 1974).

6 Hutches Trower to David Ricardo, 10 January 1822. Reprinted in Piero Sraffa (ed.), *The works and correspondence of David Ricardo* (11 vols.; Cambridge, 1951-5), ix, 145. (Italics in original).

7 Ricardo to Trower, 24 July 1823, in Sraffa (ed.), *David Ricardo,* ix, 314.
8 Ricardo to Trower, 25 Jan. 1822, in Sraffa (ed.), *David Ricardo,* ix, 153.
9 Trower to Ricardo, 10 Jan. 1822, in Sraffa (ed.), *David Ricardo,* ix, 145.
10 Quoted in Mansergh, *Irish question,* p. 64.
11 See Oliver MacDonagh's 'Irish emigration to the United States of America and the British colonies during the famine', in R. Dudley Edwards and T. Desmond Williams (eds), *The great famine: studies in Irish history 1845-52* (reprint, New York, 1976, of original ed. Dublin, 1956), pp. 319 et seq.; especially pp. 332-40 on 'Landlord-assisted emigration'.
12 Robert Kane, *The industrial resources of Ireland* (reprint, Shannon, 1971, of 2nd ed. Dublin, 1845; first ed., 1844), p. 257. See also John Pitt Kennedy, *Digest of evidence taken before Her Majesty's commissioners of inquiry into the state of the law and practice in respect to the occupation of land in Ireland* (2 vols.; Dublin, 1847), i, 563-702. Hereafter cited as *Devon digest.*
13 Kane, *Industrial resources of Ireland,* p. 308.
14 Mansergh, *Irish question,* p. 64.
15 Quoted in Mansergh, *Irish question,* p. 64. (My italics). Mill's proposals in the *Morning Chronicle* during the winter of 1846-7 were subsequently incorporated into his *Principles of political economy* (1st ed.; London, 1848), vol. i, pp. 381-400.
16 W.T. Thornton, *A plea for peasant proprietors: with the outlines of a plan for their establishment in Ireland* (London, 1848).
17 Black, *Economic thought and the Irish question,* p. 31.
18 T.P. O'Neill's 'The economic and political ideas of James Fintan Lalor', *Irish Ecclesiastical Record* vol. lxxiv (1950), pp. 398-409, is less a consideration of Lalor's economic theories than of his use of law. This article forms the basis of Chapter VI of the same author's *Fiontán Ó Leathlobhair,* pp. 39-50.
19 Advertised in the *Dublin Evening Post,* 24 July 1817; reprinted in Mac Suibhne (ed.), *Knockbeg Centenary Book,* pp. 150-1.
20 George O'Brien, 'William Conner' in *Studies,* xii, no. 46, p. 283.
21 *The true political economy of Ireland; or rack-rent, the one great cause of all her evils, with its remedy* (Dublin, 1835).
22 *The prosecuted speech delivered in proposing a petition to Parliament in favour of a valuation and a perpetuity of his farm to the tenant, with an introductory address on the nature and spirit of Toryism* (Dublin, 1842) passim.
23 Fogarty, *Lalor,* p. 22. Lalor makes abundantly clear who would receive the forfeited aristocratic lands: they '[would] be vested *in the occupying tenants'.* (My italics).
24 Fogarty, *Lalor,* p. 95; italics in original.
25 Fogarty, *Lalor,* p. 95; italics in original.
26 Lalor does not consider the most likely possibility: that 'the people' might decide to pay *no rents* whatever.

27 Fogarty, *Lalor*, p. 101; italics in original.
28 *The Nation,* 24 April 1847. Rough draft in N.L.I., MS 340; reprinted in Fogarty, *Lalor*, pp. 7-25; quotation from p. 19.
29 Fogarty, *Lalor*, p. 20.
30 Fogarty, *Lalor*, p. 21.
31 Fogarty, *Lalor*, pp. 20-21.
32 Rather than quote and analyse by turns, it seems more reasonable to quote the passage in full (long though it is) and make the necessary observations thereafter.
33 *The Nation,* 24 April 1847; reprinted in Fogarty, *Lalor*, pp. 21-4.
34 The number of occupiers is computed from the *Devon Commission* Appendix 95 (i), p. 288, H.C. 1845 (672), xxii. I have totalled the returns from columns 9 through 28 (i.e., all landholders of more than one acre), and subtracted Lalor's 'class of 8,000'.
35 Fogarty, *Lalor*, pp. 21, 23 and 24. (My italics).
36 Fogarty, *Lalor*, p. 22.
37 Rough draft of letter on 'Irish agricultural society', dated 10 Jan. 1844, N.L.I., MS 340; partly reprinted in Fogarty, *Lalor*, pp. xvii-xix. Quotation from p. xvi.
38 Fogarty, *Lalor*, p. xvii.
39 Fogarty, *Lalor*, p. xix.
40 Kane, *Industrial resources of Ireland,* p. iii.
41 Black, *Economic thought and the Irish question,* p. 134-58.
42 These were Thomas Davis' views as printed in *The Nation*, 31 Dec. 1842, 30 Sept. 1843, 2 Dec. 1843.
43 See Blackstone, *Commentaries,* ii, pp. 2, and 7-8.
44 Kane, *Industrial resources of Ireland,* pp. 251-2.
45 Adam Smith as quoted by Andrew Skinner in his introduction to *The wealth of nations* (Harmondsworth, 1974), p. 31. See also, Bk. V, Ch, I, Part I of the same work (Modern Library edition; New York, 1965, pp. 653-6). As one student remarks: 'All these discussions have in common the fact that [the] stages are regarded as a natural, obvious sequence, which requires no explanation. The factors causing transition from one stage to the next are unexplained, or assumed to be associated essentially with the general advancement of the human mind. Thus, these theories are not theories of economic stages in the strict sense, but reflections on the economic aspects of theories of human progress in general'. Bert F. Hoselitz (ed.), *Theories of Economic growth* (London, New York, 1960), p. 199n.
46 *The Nation,* 24 April 1847; reprinted in Fogarty, *Lalor*, pp. 7-25; quotation from p. 9.
47 Roger Price, *The economic modernisation of France* (London, 1975), p. 54. (My italics).
48 *Modernisation of France,* p. 44.

49 See, for example, Barrington Moore, jr., *Social origins of dictatorship and democracy: lord and peasant in the making of the modern world* (Harmondsworth, 1969), pp. 10-28.

50 Isaac Butt, 'The famine in the land. What has been done, and what is to be done', *Dublin University Magazine,* xxix, no. 172 (April 1847), pp. 501-40. See p. 506 for use of the phrase 'social economy'. See also, John Stuart Mill, *England and Ireland* (London, 1868), pp. 9, 10, 14, 19 and 22.

51 See, for example, the report of Dr Hughes' lecture on 'The condition of Ireland' in *The Nation,* 1 May 1847; and Lalor's reply on 15 May (rough draft of letter in N.L.I., MS 340). Hughes uses the phrase 'social and political economy' also. This would tend to suggest that it was a fairly common usage at the time.

52 Friedrich List, *National system of political economy* (London, 1841).

53 See Donald Winch, 'The emergence of economics as a science', in Cipolla (ed.), *Economic history of Europe*, iii, 553 et seq.

54 Eric Roll, *A history of economic thought* (2nd ed.; London, 1962), p. 135.

55 This and the previous quotation are from Joseph J. Spengler's 'Mercantilist and Physiocratic growth theory', in Hoselitz (ed.), *Theories of economic growth,* p. 55.

56 *The Nation,* 15 May 1847; Fogarty, *Lalor*, p. 26.

57 *The Nation,* 24 April 1847; Fogarty, *Lalor*, p. 13.

58 Fogarty, *Lalor*, p. 34.

59 Butt, 'The famine in the land', *Dublin University Magazine* (April 1847), later issued in pamphlet form.

60 *The Nation,* 2 January 1847.

61 Butt, 'The famine in the land', *Dublin University Magazine* (April 1847), p. 537.

62 Butt, 'The famine in the land', *Dublin University Magazine* (April 1847), p. 540.

63 John Mitchel, *The last conquest of Ireland (perhaps)*, p. 219.

64 For Lalor's view of the conditions of the 'independent labourers' see Fogarty, *Lalor,* pp. 27-8.

65 For the conditions on the five acre holdings, see Fogarty, *Lalor*, pp. 28-29, 30.

66 For Lalor's view of the five to ten acre holdings, see Fogarty, *Lalor*, pp. 28-30.

67 Fogarty, *Lalor*, p. 29.

68 Fogarty, *Lalor*, pp. 30-1.

69 Fogarty, *Lalor*, p. 31.

70 Fogarty, *Lalor*, pp. 32-3.

71 See map in Finlay Dun, *Landlords and tenants in Ireland* (London, 1881), where Coote is credited with some 47,451 statute acres.

72 Fintan to D'Arcy McGee, 30 March 1847; N.L.I., MS 340. Reprinted in Fogarty, *Lalor*, pp. xxii-xxiv; quotation from pp. xxiii-xxiv.

73 Fogarty, *Lalor*, p. 31.
74 *Devon digest,* i, 473-562.
75 See P. Lynch and J. Vaizey, *Guinness's brewery in the Irish economy 1759-1876* (Cambridge, 1960), passim; Joseph Lee, 'The dual economy in Ireland, 1800-50' in T. Desmond Williams (ed.), *Historical Studies* vii (Dublin, 1971), pp. 191-201.
76 *Devon digest*, i, 531-48.
77 *Devon digest*, i, 519 et seq.; see also T. Walsh et al., 'A half century of fertiliser and lime use in Ireland', *Journal of the statistical and social inquiry society of Ireland*, xix (1956-7), pp. 104-36.
78 *Dublin Evening Herald,* 5, 10, 14, 19, 24, and 26 Nov. 1846; 1 and 8 Dec. 1846; miscellaneous articles on 'Irish agriculture'.
79 Fogarty, *Lalor*, p. 27.
80 Fogarty, *Lalor*, p. 36.
81 Fogarty, *Lalor*, p. 10.
82 The standard, classic treatment is Raymond D. Crotty's brilliant book *Irish agricultural production: its volume and structure* (Cork, 1966); see pp. 35-107. See also Joseph Lee's incisive review 'Irish agriculture' in *Agricultural history review* xvii, no. 1 (1969), pp. 64-76.
83 See E.R.R. Green, 'Agriculture' in R. Dudley Edwards and T. Desmond Williams (eds), *The great famine,* pp. 89-128; especially pp. 123ff.
84 E.R.R.Green, 'Agriculture' in Edwards and Williams (eds), *The great famine,* p. 127.
85 Crotty, *Irish agricultural production,* pp. 35 et seq.
86 See Cormac Ó Gráda's pioneer article, 'Supply responsiveness in Irish agriculture during the nineteenth century', *Economic history review,* 2nd series, xxviii, no. 2 (1975), pp. 312-17.
87 *Returns of agricultural produce in Ireland in the year 1847: Part 1. Tillage returns,* H.C. 1847-8 (923), lvii; pp. viii-ix.
88 *The census of Ireland for the year 1851, part 2: returns of agricultural produce in 1851,* H.C. 1852-3 (1589), xciii; pp. xviii-xix.
89 E.R.R. Green, 'Agriculture' in Edwards and Williams (eds), *the great famine,* p. 124.
90 Fogarty, *Lalor* (1918 ed.), p. xxiii.

CHAPTER 5: CONCLUSION: IDENTITY AND INFLUENCE

1 No doubt F.S.L. Lyons, *Ireland since the famine* (1st ed., 1971; rev. ed. Glasgow, 1973), p. 34, was simply summarising existing scholarship when he declared that, whereas the famine had 'accelerated certain trends and intensified certain problems' (p. 34), it could not, for all that, be regarded as a watershed in Irish history, 'at least in any meaningful sense' (Crotty, *Irish agricultural production,* p. 46). A comparison of Ó Tuathaigh's *Ireland before*

the famine (1972), pp. 203-27, with Lee's *Modernisation of Irish society* (1973), pp. 1-35, may suggest the consensus was either short-lived or overestimated. Misplaced literalism aside, the famine clearly remains the primary locus of inquiry into nineteenth-century Ireland and recent scholarship reflects that fact. See, for instance, Kerby A. Miller's *Emigrants and Exiles. Ireland and the Irish Exodus to North America* (Oxford, 1985), which might with justice be subtitled 'The Oxford history of Irish emigration'! Almost two thirds of the book (Chs 6, 7, and 8; pp. 193-555), uses the famine as a datum. See also Joel Mokyr's *Why Ireland starved: a quantitative and analytical history of the Irish economy, 1800-1850* (London, 1983), and Kevin O'Neill's incisive critque in *The Irish Literary Supplement,* Spring, 1984. Mokyr's work is best read in conjunction with Cormac Ó Gráda's recent collection of essays, *Ireland before and after the famine. Explorations in economic history, 1800-1925* (Manchester, 1988). Though no less 'sophisticated' in his approach or impatient in his judgements, Ó Gráda has a greater respect for the 'integrity' of the past.

2 *Irish Felon,* 1 July 1848; reprint of letter dated 25 January 1847. Fogarty, *Lalor*, p. 81.
3 *The Nation,* 24 April 1847; in Fogarty, *Lalor*, pp. 16 and 11 respectively.
4 *The Nation,* 24 April 1847 and *Irish Felon,* 24 June 1848; in Fogarty, *Lalor*, pp. 12 and 61 respectively.
5 Thomas P. O'Neill, 'The economic and political ideas of James Fintan Lalor' in the *Irish Ecclesiastical Record,* lxxiv (Nov. 1950), p. 404. See also the same author's *Fiontán Ó Leathlobhair,* pp. 39-50.
6 *Irish Felon,* 1 July 1848, 'To the Confederate and Repeal Clubs in Ireland'; rough draft in N.L.I., MS 340. Reprinted in Fogarty, *Lalor*, pp. 67-83; quotations from pp. 70, 74 and 81 respectively. (Italics in original).
7 *Irish Felon.* 8 July 1848; in Fogarty, *Lalor*, p. 104.
8 George Woodcock, *The anarchist reader* (Glasgow, 1977), p. 15. See also George Woodcock, *Anarchism* (Harmondsworth, 1975); Irving L. Horowitz (ed.), *The anarchists* (New York, 1964), pp. 28-55; and James Joll, *The anarchists* (London, 1964).
9 *The Nation,* 24 April 1847; in Fogarty, *Lalor*, pp. 12 and 14.
10 Woodcock, *The anarchist reader,* p. 11.
11 Woodcock, *The anarchist reader*, p. 15; *The Nation,* 24 April 1847; in Fogarty, *Lalor*, pp. 13-14, and 20 especially.
12 *The Nation,* 24 April 1847; Fogarty, *Lalor*, p. 12.
13 E.R. Norman, *A history of modern Ireland* (London, 1971), p. 131.
14 Richard Hofstadter, *The American political tradition and the men who made it* (New York, 1973), p. 34.
15 As Ó Tuathaigh (*Ireland before the famine,* p. 200) correctly points out, it was not until *after* the outbreak of the February Revolution in Paris that 'Meagher and Mitchel . . . raised the cry for an Irish republic, [this being] the first time a

republic had been suggested in Repeal circles'.

16 Jefferson, quoted in Hofstadter's, *American political tradition,* p. 35.

17 The percentage given here refers to the proportion of repeal M.P.s who were also lawyers.

18 George Lichteim, *A short history of socialism* (Glasgow, 1975), p. 15.

19 *Irish Felon,* 1 July 1848; in Fogarty, *Lalor*, p. 75.

20 See Thomas Paine, *Rights of man*, edited by Henry Collins (Harmondsworth, 1969), pp. 105, 128, and 165.

21 See Isaac Kramnick's introduction to Thomas Paine, *Common sense* (Harmondsworth, 1976), pp. 46-55.

22 Elie Halevy, *The growth of philosophical radicalism* (Boston, 1965).

23 See Raymond Williams, *Keywords*, pp. 209-11.

24 Lichteim, *A short history of socialism,* pp. 378-9.

25 Kevin B. Nowlan, *The politics of repeal: a study in the relations between Great Britain and Ireland, 18451-50* (London, 1965), p. 230.

26 Duffy, *Four years of Irish history,* pp. 476-7.

27 Duffy, *Four years of Irish history,* p. 491.

28 Lee, *Modernisation of Irish society,* p. 2.

29 Despite the force and intelligence which he brought to the task of legitimising tenant grievances, and the ruthless manner in which he used the Confederation to force the issue onto the political stage, the standard work on the Tenant Right League merely glosses over Lalor's contribution to that movement. See J.H. Whyte, *The Independent Irish Party, 1850-9* (Oxford, 1958), p. 5 et seq.

30 Desmond Ryan, *The phoenix flame: a study in fenianism and John Devoy* (London, 1937), p. 319.

31 Michael Davitt, *The fall of feudalism in Ireland* (London, 1904), p. 82.

32 T.A. Jackson, *Ireland her own: an outline history of the Irish struggle* (London, 1976), p. 321.

33 Lyons, *Ireland since the famine*, p. 163.

34 Paul Bew, *Land and the national question in Ireland, 1858-82* (Dublin, 1978), p. 48. See also T.W. Moody, *Davitt and Irish revolution, 1846-82* (Oxford, 1981), pp. 237-40.

35 Davitt, *The fall of feudalism in Ireland,* pp. 149-50. See also, Moody, *Davitt and Irish revolution,* pp. 284-6, and 288-92.

36 Davitt, *The fall of feudalism in Ireland,* p. 160. Moody, *Davitt and Irish revolution,* pp. 316-18.

37 O'Hanlon, O'Leary and Lalor, *History of the Queen's County,* ii, 732; Moody, *Davitt and Irish revolution,* pp. 367, 419.

38 O'Hanlon, O'Leary and Lalor, *History of the Queen's County,* ii, 728.

39 Moody suggests that Davitt *first came into contact with Lalor's ideas* in September 1878 at the Cooper Institute (New York) meeting, but that he probably *first read* Lalor in 1880. See, *Davitt and Irish revolution,* pp. 233-4 (re Cooper Institute), and p. 208.

Bibliography

In a study such as this — given more to reinterpreting than to reconstructing the past — debts to existing scholarship are, inevitably, extensive. I have therefore relied rather heavily on footnotes, both to itemize my debts and to explain my differences on particular issues. Since full citations are available in the appropriate footnotes, and since lack of space precludes re-citation here of all the primary and secondary sources consulted, what follows is but a select list of those that proved most useful in researching this work.

Any evaluation of Lalor's life, times and troubles must, perforce, begin with his personal papers (MS 340), and with the Lalor family papers (MSS 8562-8575), both housed in the National Library in Dublin. For his father's politics and career in the 1830s, the primary sources are the *Second report of the Select Committee of the House of Lords appointed to enquire into the collection and payment of tithes in Ireland,* H.L. 1831-32 (663), xxii; and, the *Second report from the Select Committee of the House of Commons appointed to enquire into the collection and payment of tithes in Ireland 1831-2,* (508), xxi. Additional local detail can be gleaned from *The Leinster Express* and *The Leinster Leader,* especially during election years; and also from Revd J. Canon O'Hanlon, Revd E. O'Leary, and Revd M. Lalor, *History of the Queen's County* (2 vols., Dublin, 1907-14).

For Fintan himself, Maurice Lenihan's 'Reminiscences of a journalist' in the *Limerick Reporter and Tipperary Vindicator*, 1866, 1867, and 1870, are invaluable. Something of his early ideas can be gleaned from the numerous pamphlets of his mentor, William Conner: *The speech of William Conner Esq., against rackrents, etc.* (Dublin, 1832); *The true political economy of Ireland; or rack-rent the one great cause of all her evils, with its remedy* (Dublin, 1835); *The axe laid to the root of Irish oppression* (Dublin, 1840); *The prosecuted speech delivered in proposing a petition to Parliament in favour of a valuation and a perpetuity of his farm to the tenant, etc.* (Dublin, 1842); *A letter to the tenantry of Ireland containing an exposition of the rackrent system* (Dublin, 1850); and, *The catechism of valuation and perpetuity of tenure* (3rd ed.; Dublin, 1850). For the source of Fintan's legal arguments see William Blackstone's *Commentaries on the laws of England* 4 vols. (15th ed.; London, 1809).

The use to which he put these and other ideas can be readily gleaned from any of the following convenient collections: L. Fogarty, *James Fintan Lalor: patriot and political essayist: 1807-1849* (Dublin, 1918; 2nd ed. Dublin, 1947); Nathaniel Marlowe (ed.), *James Fintan Lalor: collected writings* (Dublin, 1918); or T.J. O'Donohue (ed.), *The writings of James Fintan Lalor: with an introduction embodying personal recollections by John O'Leary* (Dublin, 1895). The natural context of these ideas can best be gauged by a perusal of contemporary newspapers, especially the O' Connellite *Freeman's Journal* and *The Pilot,* Young Ireland's *The Nation,* Mitchel's combative *United Irishman,* and Brennan's equally confrontational *Irish Felon.* For the broader context of discourse and debate the following collections also proved useful: W.J. Fitzpatrick (ed.), *Correspondence of Daniel O' Connell, the Liberator* (2 vols.; London, 1888); L. Fogarty, *Father John Kenyon, a patriot priest of forty-eight* (Dublin, n.d.); Arthur Griffith (ed.), *Meagher of the sword. Speeches of Thomas Francis Meagher in Ireland 1846-8* (Dublin, 1917); and T.W. Rolleston (ed.), *Prose writings of Thomas Davis* (London, n.d.). The heterogeneity of opinions and opinion-makers among the Young Irelanders is clearly reflected in the early compilation *The voice of the Nation; a manual of nationality* (Dublin, 1844), whilst 'official' Irish opinion on the major issues of the day is paraded in the *Reports of the Parliamentary Committee of the Loyal National Repeal Association* (3 vols.; Dublin, 1844-6). British opinion on Irish matters is probably accurately reflected in *Hansard's Parliamentary Debates,* 3rd series.

The economic and social background of the period is voluminously documented in various parliamentary reports and commissions. For the 1830s, see the *Reports of the commission for inquiring into the condition of the poorer classes in Ireland* H.C., 1835 (309) xxxii; 1836 (35), (43) xxx; 1836 (36) xxxi; 1836 (37) xxxii; 1836 (38) xxxiii; 1836 (39) (40) (41) xxxiv; 1837 (68) xxxi. For the 1840s, the best official source is the *Report from H.M. Commissioners of inquiry into the state of the law and practice in respect to the occupation of land in Ireland* H.C. 1845, (605), (606), xix; (616), xx; (657), xxi; (672) (673), xxii, conveniently summarised in John Pitt Kennedy's *Digest of evidence taken before Her Majesty's commissioners of inquiry into the state of the law and practice in respect to the occupation of land in Ireland* (2 vols.; Dublin, 1847). For the statistical background, see the *Report of the commissioners appointed to take the census of Ireland for the year 1841* H.C. 1843 (504), xxiv; and, for an early and interesting attempt to analyse such recalcitrant materials, see Francis Dowdall's articles on 'Irish Agriculture' in the *Dublin Evening Post* (Nov. and Dec., 1846). This approach was made considerably easier thereafter by the regular publication of the *Returns of agricultural produce in Ireland.* I have relied in particular on the tillage returns for 1847, available in H.C. 1847-8 (923), lvii, and on *The census of Ireland for the year 1851, part 2: returns of agricultural produce in 1851,* H.C. 1852-3 (1589), xciii. On the famine, Charles E. Trevelyan's bureaucratic detachment in *The Irish crisis* (London, 1848), may fruitfully be compared with Isaac Butt's alarmed despair in *A voice for Ireland. The famine in the land* (Dublin, London, 1847).

As the history of the period was first written by Lalor's contemporaries and political heirs, their memoirs also prove especially valuable. Of particular interest here is the prolific output of Charles Gavan Duffy: *Four Years of Irish history, 1845-1849,* (London, 1883); *Young Ireland: a fragment of Irish history, 1840-5,* (Dublin, 1884); *The league of north and south: an episode in Irish history, 1850-4* (London, 1886); *My life in two hemispheres* (London, 1888); and, *Thomas Davis, the memoirs of an Irish patriot, 1840-6* (London, 1890). John Mitchel gives his version of events in both *The last conquest of Ireland (perhaps)* (Glasgow, n.d.), and in *Jail Journal, or five years in British jails* (Dublin, 1913; ed. by Arthur Griffith). John O'Leary, *Recollections of fenians and fenianism* (2 vols., London, 1896), shows how little the fenians actually owed to Lalor, whilst Michael Davitt's *The fall of feudalism in Ireland* (London, 1904), uses Fintan's (recently resuscitated) reputation to legitimize his own position in the Land War. See also, Davitt's *The rise of the Irish movement* (Dublin, 1910). James Connolly deals extensively with Lalor's ideas in his introduction to *The rights of Ireland and the faith of a felon by James Fintan Lalor* (Dublin, n.d.), and in his wonderful later work, *Labour in Irish History,* (Dublin, 1910). For P.H. Pearse's hagiographic interpretation see *The murder machine and other essays* (Cork, 1976).

Of secondary works, by far the most important are Tomás Ó Néill's standard biography, *Fiontán Ó Leathlobhair* (Dublin, 1962) and his scattered articles: 'The papers of James Fintan Lalor in the National Library', *The Irish Book Lover,* xxx (Jan. 1948); 'Fintan Lalor and the 1849 movement', *An Cosantóir: the Irish defence journal,* x, no. 4 (April, 1950); 'The economic and political ideas of James Fintan Lalor', *Irish Ecclesiastical Record,* vol. lxxiv (Nov. 1950); and, 'James Fintan Lalor' in J.W. Boyle (ed.), *Leaders and workers* (Cork, 1966). For the dominant political movement of the period, see Kevin B. Nowlan's *The politics of repeal: a study in the relations between Great Britain and Ireland, 1841-50* (London, 1965). There is, as yet, no comprehensive treatment of Young Ireland which adequately deals with its complexity, though M.J. MacManus (ed.), *Thomas Davis and Young Ireland* (Dublin, 1945), provides a useful starting point. See also Mary Buckley's *Thomas Davis, a study in nationalist philosophy* (unpublished Ph.D., U.C.C., 1980), and R. Davis' recent account of *The Young Ireland Movement* (Dublin, 1987). For later political movements the following proved most useful: J.H. Whyte, *The Independent Irish Party, 1850-9* (Oxford, 1958); T.W. Moody (ed.), *The fenian movement* (Cork, 1968); Desmond Ryan, *The phoenix flame: a study of fenianism and John Devoy* (London, 1937); Paul Bew, *Land and the national question in Ireland, 1858-82* (Dublin, 1978); and T.W. Moody's *Davitt and Irish revolution, 1846-82* (Oxford, 1981). Electoral fortunes throughout the century have been conveniently charted in B.M. Walker (ed.), *Parliamentary election results in Ireland, 1801-1922* (Dublin, 1978).

On economic and social issues, T.W. Freedman's *Pre-famine Ireland. A study in historical geography* (Manchester, 1957), surveys the country in 1841, whilst R. Dudley Edwards and T. Desmond Williams (eds), *The great famine: studies in Irish history 1845-52* (Dublin, 1956), is a comprehensive assessment of the 'great divide'. Joseph Lee's essays on 'Irish agriculture', *Agricultural history review* xvii, no. 1 (1969), pp. 64-76, and on 'The dual economy in Ireland, 1800-45', in T. Desmond Williams (ed.), *Historical studies,* vii (Dublin, 1971), pp. 191-201, also proved useful. Economic theories and policies on a variety of Irish issues are ably surveyed in R.D. Collison Black's *Economic thought and the Irish question, 1817-70*

(Cambridge, 1960). Nicholas Mansergh's *The Irish question 1840-1921* (3rd ed.; London, 1975), provides a useful corrective to *Marx/Engels: Ireland and the Irish question* (Moscow, London, 1978), which shamelessly parades the inability of classical Marxism to deal with 'the question' of Ireland. On the broader, but related, issue of class, Patricia Hollis (ed.), *Class and class conflict in nineteenth-century England 1815-50* (London, 1973), is excellent both as a sourcebook of primary materials and as an interpretative essay. Harold Perkin's *Origins of modern English society* (London, 1969), is a pæan to industrialization, warts and all, in the neighbouring isle; whilst E.P. Thompson's stimulating polemic, *The making of the English working class* (Harmondsworth, 1968), has less to do with class than with a self-evident 'Englishness' — which probably explains why it is so abominable on the Irish.

On the vexed question of Lalor's legal arguments I relied on the following: A.V. Dicey, *Law and opinion in England during the nineteenth century* (London, 1905); F.W. Maitland and F.C. Montague, *A sketch of English legal history* (New York, 1951); Carl Joachim Friedrich, *The philosophy of law in historical perspective* (2nd ed.; Chicago, London, 1963); J. Walter Jones, *Historical introduction to the theory of law* (Oxford, 1940); and Lawrence C. Becker's *Property rights: philosophic foundations* (London, 1977).

Of the remaining secondary materials two, in particular, deserve special notice: Oliver MacDonagh's *Ireland: the Union and its aftermath* (London, 1977), is a scintillating essay to which all students are indebted; and Raymond D. Crotty's seminal work *Irish agricultural production: its volume and structure* (Cork, 1966), is a wide-ranging critique of traditional historiography and the misguided policies it has spawned. Among textbooks, though J.C. Beckett's *The making of modern Ireland, 1603-1923* (London, 1966) and F.S.L. Lyons' *Ireland since the famine* (Glasgow, 1971), still hold pride of place, I found Gearóid Ó Tuathaig's *Ireland before the famine: 1798-1848* (Dublin, 1972), less encyclopedic and more engaging. For the post-famine period, Joseph Lee's provocative (if untenable) thesis, *The modernisation of Irish society: 1848-1918* (Dublin, 1973), stimulatingly demonstrates that historians may *have* ideas as well as report them.

Index